You Will Make It...
Just Keep Going

Stephanie Reef

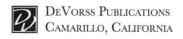
DeVorss Publications
Camarillo, California

You Will Make It...Just Keep Going
Copyright © 2020
by Stephanie Reef

First published in 2020 by Stephanie Reef
First DeVorss Publications Edition, 2023
ISBN Print: 9780875169293
ISBN eBook: 9780875169309

DeVorss & Company, Publisher
PO Box 1389
Camarillo CA 93012
editorial@devorss.com

Printed in the United States of America
For more information, please visit www.devorss.com

Editor's note: Due to the clairaudient (channeled) content presented in
this book, many rules of writing have been disregarded. Clairaudience
is the ability to receive an intuitive spoken message from the world of
spirits or higher sources.

This book is dedicated to
those who are lost amongst the chaos
and feel like just giving up.

You CAN and WILL make it . . .

I promise.

One day at a time . . .
One Message at a time . . .
One thought at a time . . .
One breath at a time . . .

. . . Just Keep Going

Contents

The Preface

What if you were given a chance to live the life you've only dreamt about? A life without any restrictions or limitations, including money? What would that life look like?

Really think about this before you answer. Don't just look on the surface of your reality now, but go deep within your heart and soul. Because I can say this with confidence: Many of us are not living the life that resonates with who we truly are.

We have ultimately settled in some form—if not all—for the most part, because we have either felt unworthy of living the way we want or compelled to live as others see fit, including God. Remember, the only plan that God has for you is the plan that comes from your heart.

Your Creator will give you ANYTHING that comes from the heart. The only problem is when our head hits our heart, it causes confusion and uncertainty.

It is then that we wonder why we aren't living the

life we desire. Our existence becomes that of contradiction and throws everything out of balance, causing illness, poverty, discord and unhappiness. When we live as to what is in our hearts—truly live—without any fear or refrainment, it is only then our lives become miraculously abundant.

I ask that you sit still for a moment in the peaceful quiet. Relax your body and release all from your mind. Breathe consciously and look through your mind's eye. Envision a key that is unlocking the door to your heart. What do you see inside? What kind of person are you? What kind of life is deep within your soul? When you really discover the answers to those questions, begin to solely focus on what comes to the forefront of your thoughts. Then you will know what your life should authentically look like.

Don't be afraid of what you see. Instead, embrace it and soon your life will begin to change according to your thoughts. Know this: When you open your heart and allow what's in there to come out, the Universe and the Creator will begin to rearrange your life and all that's around you in order to create the authentic life you were meant to live.

With that said, be prepared. For change can come gently like a lamb or strong like a lion. It may sway the boat a bit or tip it completely over.

It is when we invite change into our life, our world can instantly be turned upside down and shaken.

Don't panic when this happens. This is a good thing. Instead, embrace it and ride the wave for it is taking you to great heights. God knows what you want and, most importantly, what you can handle.

Know this, we all have the power to manifest ANYTHING we desire without the need for money or material exchange as we are accustomed to. We as co-creators with a Higher Power, can build within our MINDS the perfect life. This power I speak of is called INTENTION. This is WORD and/or LAW.

Throughout this book you will obtain bits of knowledge that will help you to understand the process. Stay focused and open; for if you really pay attention, you can have a brand new life that you've always wanted within days.

How do I know this to be true? I am the living proof.

…Just Keep Going.

The Introduction

None of us are immune to the difficulties and challenges of life here on Earth. We all experience heartache, loss, illness, fear, uncertainty and disconnection during the course of our lifetimes.

And it is during these dark moments that we find ourselves questioning life itself;

How did this happen?

Why am I going through this?

When will this end?

What do I do now?

Yet, if you really think about it, the true question that is being asked here is:

"Am I going to make it?"

And I say;

"Yes...you will."

Why? Because "You are worthy." It took me years—along with much heartache and discord—not only to understand this, but embrace it, then live it.

Early in my life, I acquired a belief that I wouldn't

amount to much and would struggle immensely, resulting in destitution and defeat. I held on to this belief, giving credibility and weight to it.

I didn't know that I had a choice to believe it or not, based on my own understanding. This one belief—I carried for so long—created such devastation, resulting in divorce, abandonment, homelessness, poverty and illness. The depression, anxiety and worthlessness I felt, led to many addictions and eventually the desire to end it all.

It wasn't until that fateful day, when I experienced something I couldn't explain nor deny that would miraculously change my life.

As of today, the Presence is still with me. However, I know now, it always has been, walking with me every step of the way along this journey called life.

The book you are holding is filled with motivation, inspiration and a bit of tough love.

These are the Messages I received through my clairaudience on my path to self-discovery and self-healing.

My hope is that these Messages will help you find your way back....

Back to a place once forgotten. A place where you felt strength, peace and a sense of true faith, knowing that you were created to live a powerful life...

Right here.

Right now.

But know this, I said "powerful," not comfortable, safe or easy. In fact, living a powerful life is far from what you would think. The terrain can be rough, daunting and overwhelming. It can bring you to your knees, showing no mercy while turning your world upside down when you least expect it.

But in the end, when you have forged through, you will come to a place that is visited by few and will experience a certain greatness that goes beyond any success or achievement that is assumed by many without true sacrifice.

This book's sole purpose is to help you to "just keep going" during these turbulent moments while on the battlefield of life or when you feel like giving up and just need some kind of direction.

The book isn't about becoming a successful person; it's about becoming a better human which inevitably will make you a success within your own right as you navigate through this life here on earth.

Know this: You are not alone.

The Presence is with you and there to co-create with you to manifest all that you so desire. You must understand: The very life that you envision having—your Creator sees an even grander one and will help you to attain as such. "Ask and it shall be given." Always.

For what you desire, is already within you. It is already yours. Right here.

And with that, we acquire a faith that is unshakable, knowing that we have the power within us to change ANY and ALL circumstances as we choose. No matter how bad things may be right now...

...Just Keep Going

SEE these words in your mind.

SPEAK them every time you feel the desire to give up.

HEAR them every time you're faced with adversity.

KNOW them with every fiber of your being.

And I promise, you will not only get through, you will make it another day...and then another.

Remember, when we speak the words "And it is so I become what I have just spoken," we create motion within the physical realm that allows for what we have just said to come TRUE.

...Just Keep Going

The Beginning

I awoke—once again—to the gut wrenching emptiness I'd felt inside for some time. The faint morning light, etching its way through the window, reminding me another day had come. Another day, I'd have to muster enough strength just to get through.

It wasn't the first time the desire to leave this Earth brushed across my thoughts. I was living in a hell that no one knew about, surrounded by others who were experiencing Heaven at the same time. No matter how hard I tried, nothing worked. I felt cursed, alone and destined for a life of failure. Some say during those dark moments, time suspends and begins to loop—replaying those dreadful thoughts over and over—taking captive of the very core of your mind.

In the midst of my hopelessness, I laid there, trying to encase myself within the blankets, wanting nothing more than to close my eyes, never to awake.

However, this time was different, for I felt a strange Presence poking at my mind, as if—almost—supernatural. As I worked to shake my sleepiness, the nudge became persistent, pelting me to get my attention, like an annoying drip coming from the ceiling. Only then did I realize I wasn't alone, not just in the room, but in the world and beyond.

The Presence was that of peace, comfort and reassurance. The stronger it got, the more it seemed to have a certain intellect and profound knowing.

At that very moment, a peculiar shift within my reality occurred and for the first time, I was given a glimpse of the possibility of Heaven. It was then I knew, everything was okay, including me. I heard the words clearly spoken in my mind. All I had to do was;

...Just Keep Going

The One Truth

There is but ONE TRUTH to live by in order to have a life that one could only ever truly imagine living. And that is;

You must THINK of yourself as God THINKS of you. And that is PERFECT, like God.

Which ultimately means:

Your health is PERFECT despite otherwise.

Your wealth is PERFECT despite otherwise.

Your relationships are PERFECT despite otherwise.

Your entire life is PERFECT despite otherwise.

You must THINK and BELIEVE everything is PERFECT not only as God is, but as God sees you to be.

Then, and only then, will you and your life become PERFECT as God intended.

This is the ONE TRUTH...The Only Truth.

What is Your Story?
Your story is to reflect the Truth.

I dare you to go beyond all limits to imagine the story you were truly meant to live.

The Journey

You are about to embark on a journey that many steer clear of. And that is, the road leading to change. Those who elude this inevitable, yet unchartered terrain, usually settle for a mediocre existence. They would rather endure then evolve. But it is when we can no longer tolerate our circumstances that we willingly invite change into our lives.

It is then that we experience a shift within our reality as the "old" energy breaks loose and begins to dissipate, allowing the "new" energy to take form to create a new reality. This, we call;

"Evolution"

We begin to understand that it is not our circumstances nor surroundings we need to change, but only ourselves, by evolving instead of resisting. We learn to adapt.

And by that, we no longer go against the grain by fighting nature itself, thus allowing for all energy to freely flow without obstruction of any kind.

This is how "miracles"—as some would call them—begin to manifest. When we allow all energy within us and around us to flow effortlessly by being authentic to who we are, then life becomes easy and abundant. It is only us, who get in the way and block this energy, creating negative static by not living our truth.

And what is truth?

Truth is the realization that we were made in the image of our Creator, which ultimately means we were meant to live healthy, prosperous and fulfilling lives now and forever. We just need to know this and more importantly, embrace it with authenticity and self-worthiness.

Within this book are Messages that will help you rediscover and embrace the Truth, a vital aspect of life that has been forgotten. It will validate what you know to be true in your heart. With that, you will begin to experience health, wealth and success like never before.

All you have to do is be open and consistent when doing the work ahead. Then, and only then, will your life change miraculously.

How to Read This Book

First, as you hold the book closed with both hands, think about the Message you would like to receive that will answer or help you with any situation.

Second, open the book to any random page that feels right to uncover a Message on the right and a daily affirmation on the left. This is the Message you need to receive at this moment.

That's it.

For when you find yourself lost, hopeless and discouraged, desperately seeking a quick lifeline to grab hold of, it is then you discover the answer you have been looking for within ONE turn of a page.

Many keep the book close at hand so they can receive a Message at any given moment or share Messages with others. Remember, you are not alone. The Presence is with everyone, walking alongside each one of us, offering help during those dark moments of uncertainty.

The Messages are Simple

The moment each Message finds you it may seem meaningless at first. Before you understand the powerful spark of each Message, it is very important to understand that once you have received it, you must express gratitude for that life-changing Message.

Thank You
Thank You
Thank You

Acknowledge Gratitude

For abundance of any kind to come our way, we must be grateful for anything that helps us along the way. The more we have gratitude, the more we will receive.

Say "thank you" every day at least 20 times and watch what happens.

Never discard any Message that you receive because you don't understand it or it doesn't seem to relate to your need. With time, when you least expect it, an epiphany will grace its presence, offering you clarity amongst the fog.

Sometimes you will get the same Message over and over. When this happens, take heed as to what is being said. Also, if you open the book to a page that is not a Message, read what is there and try to understand as to what is being said. Then close the book and try it again to receive another Message.

Silence and Solitude

When asking for a Message to come through, it is always recommended to sit quietly for a moment, clear your thoughts of any unwanted noise, breathe and let go. In this moment of pure quiet thought, you are able to connect with Spirit and experience a world beyond this one that will provide you with all you desire to know.

Working with Affirmations

Once you have received your Message, it's time to do The Work. You will find an affirmation to the left of the Message.

Affirmations are declarations of either statements or beliefs. They're positive in nature and, if spoken repeatedly, will invoke an energetic shift within the human psyche and energy field. This ripple effect causes initial movement in order to impress the subconscious mind with the desired statement.

Once settled in, the affirmation begins to take root. From there, the subconscious mind accepts the new belief as "truth," thus restructuring the outer energy and eventually, the material reality to match the new belief.

Sound confusing? You're not alone. For some, affirmations are a daunting enigma that most of the time seem futile and a waste of time. However, this is far from the truth.

Affirmations are Powerful

If you are struggling with your current reality and you're not sure how to move the energy in order to create change, begin using affirmations immediately.

The more you use them, the greater the shift. It is recommended that you speak the affirmation several times throughout the day, and most importantly, before bed. You can speak, write or draw your affirmations. Know this: EVERYTHING that you write down will manifest itself as you move forward in life.

This is why we are taught and encouraged to write out our goals. By writing it down, we are putting it into our subconscious mind. However you choose to accomplish this, just make sure they are specific and consistent.

It is important to understand that your subconscious doesn't know the difference between what is real and what is imagined. And with that, you are given the power to create miraculous change. You have the power to move mountains.

Remember, you have what it takes within you to create change. You are not alone, for the Presence is with you, leading you in the right direction, always.

Know this: There is a simple, yet powerful secret within the pages of this book to obtaining all that you desire in order to live a life you have only imagined.

When you are ready, the page will show itself to you, but only when you are ready.

The Right Message Will Find You

This book is unlike any other for, it offers direction, guidance and reassurance with just ONE turn of a page to receive an INTUITIVE Message that will answer your most pressing questions. It will give you what you need immediately, without having to read page upon page to find what you're looking for. The right Message will find you.

There is no need to dog-ear or mark any of the pages, for the Message is only good for that day. You will feel the ENERGY when you receive a Message for the first time. But only then, does the energy dissipate after the Message is received.

Meditate on the Message

Visualize, speak, and contemplate the Affirmation for just that day until a new Message is chosen for the next. It is best to work on ONE Message at a time until you feel confident that you have created the change you desire.

Now close the book, be still, quiet your mind and feel your heart.

Open the book to the page that speaks to you.

You Will Make It...
Just Keep Going

The Messages

"I love all, therefore when I see everyone and everything through the eyes of love, my life becomes love as with all that surrounds me."

I Am Love

Speak the word love to anything negative…and it will magically disappear. When you are faced with a negative situation or person, silently say; "I love all" over and over, then watch what happens. Say "I love all" to everything and everyone and I promise you will be in paradise.

Now understand, this is not about RELATION-SHIP love as most would assume. This is about a deep unexplainable love that JUST IS. Many fall short in understanding this kind of LOVE.

It is when we finally understand that love is the very fabric of life itself that do we experience change not only in our lives, but in the world as we know it.

Love is not what you believe
it to be. It is not something you
can describe. You feel it and
know it to be true.

"I am growing better every day because I am making an effort to better myself, no matter how insignificant it may seem."

I Am Improvement

If you were to leave this world today, would you be pleased in how you lived your life up until this point? If no, how could you change that right now?

The only reason you are here is to become better, thus the world becomes better. Ask yourself this: "What could I do right now, to better myself and my life?

Remember, it can be as SIMPLE as smiling more. It can be as EASY as dressing up more. It can be as FUN as being relaxed more. Or it can be BIGGER than you could imagine.

We must not wait for better circumstances or conditions In order to better ourselves. For we surely will be waiting an eternity.

You are always better today than you were yesterday. And you will be better tomorrow than you are today.

"I change any and all illusions
with just my thoughts, which
in turn changes anything
and everything around me."

I Am Illusion

Everything is an illusion within your mind. If you want to change the illusion, change your thoughts right now. Truthfully, it is that easy.

Remember, your reality changes when you change, not the other way around. Reality only conditions you.

Envision yourself as you wish to see yourself in your daily life. Keep this vision in the forefront of your mind and know that eventually, you will become that person you see.

It is for our understanding that nothing shall remain the same forever. With this knowledge we are able to better accept our current life knowing that it will change. We just need to believe that at any given moment. Always.

You are more than the person you see
in the mirror, for that is only the illusion
your mind has created today.

"My thoughts guide my life.
For me to worry about
what others think is self-
defeating and a waste of
my precious time."

I Am Assurance

If you really want to SUCCEED in life…If you really want to be HAPPY…If you really want to PROSPER…then stop caring about what others think of you or anything else for that matter.

You will never reach great heights if you are looking back to see if others are giving you the OK. Know that you have exactly what it takes to do exactly what you CHOOSE to do.

Why on Earth should we spend any energy wondering what others are thinking about us? Besides, most aren't thinking much about anything…anyway, let alone about us.

You couldn't care
less what others think about you
because you are not them. You are you.

"Better things are coming my way because I know that change is possible and I completely embrace it with a positive attitude and mindset."

I Am Transition

Nothing gets worse. It just changes. When your situation gets bad, it just means something better is making its way to you.

Stop resisting the discomfort you are experiencing. If you remain calm and still, the transition will come quickly and painlessly. Stay focused and believe that great things are coming to you.

Remember, everyone experiences the bad, the good, the ugly and the beautiful throughout life. This keeps us from becoming bored and settling for less than.

It is when we are able to stay centered during any situation or experience, knowing that it will always change, that we become immune to the emotional dysfunction that the collective creates.

You have the ability
to see the future by
looking at your present.

"I am in love with my SELF first,
without any approval needed
of any kind from anyone else.
It is then that I have the
capability of loving others."

I Am Self-Love

Truly loving yourself means just that…"SELF." Why? Because when you love yourself, you will never need any validation to confirm what you already know.

Self-love is not about conceit or ego. It's about loving yourself as God loves you, unconditionally without any agenda or motive. When you love yourself, you are saying to the world, "I am confident in who I am and I remain strong, healthy, prosperous and joyful because of that."

When we love ourselves—the true self within—we need absolutely no reassurance, and when that happens, we may begin loving others as they would want us to love them.

You are all that you need to love.

"I am worthy of being here and living an abundant, fulfilling life, for I know that when I feel self-worth, I become worthy."

I Am Worthiness

Your Creator believes you are worthy and knows your worth.

That's all that matters. If you have no self-worth, then you have nothing.

How can your Creator give you all that you desire, if you don't believe you are worthy?

When you feel unworthy deep within, everything around you fails because you feel undeserving.

If you get nothing else from this book, get this! Your self-worth is the only thing capable of making your life hell or creating the Heaven you so desire.

When we believe we are worthy of ANYTHING and EVERY-THING, only then does the world become ours.

What is it going to take
to believe you are worthy?
You were not designed to be worthless.

"I am a success because I refuse to give up for any reason. Therefore, I can fearlessly take on any challenges in life that jeopardize the very core of my being."

I Am Determination

It is when you realize giving up is no longer an option, does success prevail and become possible.

Hold tight. Stand strong. Be vigilant. Walk forward with faith and determination. You can and will make it.

It is only natural to feel like giving up. I have done it many times, and still do. But what I have learned, is that giving up affirms that I am not strong enough, that I am weak.

So, I get up, dust myself off and keep going. And for you…you CAN and you WILL too, for this moment is yours. Don't discard it like trash.

Know that all of us, at one point or another, feel like we can't or don't want to continue. Just keep going.

Your desire to give up is only your
lack of knowledge and belief in what
you can accomplish.

"I am guided with precision because I know exactly what I want and where I want to go, which helps me make sound decisions."

I Am Precision

When you doubt, you confuse. When you confuse, you stop the natural flow of the good coming to you. This is LAW. Universal Law.

Remember, everything is a learning experience. Do not hesitate, just move forward one step at a time. You will be guided as long as you listen and pay attention.

Know this: Everyone is equipped with a natural guidance system within their natural bodies. Immediately cease relying on outside sources.

When we become dependent on things that are outside of us, we lose our God given, intuitive ability to discern what is and what isn't. We give up an amazing gift that will never fail us…EVER.

You are the inner voice within.
It's time to start listening
to yourself.

"I have magical powers and remember how to use them, which enables me to remember how to create the life I desire."

I Am Magic

You are more than you think you are. Don't waste you anymore. Keep that in mind as you read this.

What if you were told you had magical powers? How would you live your life now?

Guess what? You have magical powers. You have the power to attract anything you desire into your life just by thinking and feeling it. That is your magic wand. Your God-given wand.

Start right now. By thinking about what we want, feeling it in our heart, and seeing it in our mind's eye, we can wave our hands around the air and proclaim, "It is done."

Your magic powers will only
become real when you begin
to believe they are real.

"I remain silent if I have
no words of encouragement
for others, knowing that what
I speak of another is a reflection
of myself in some way."

I Am Silent

What you speak creates an energy that surrounds you and your reality, attracting and attaching other energies that are that of the like. Be vigilant in the words that come out of your mouth. Always.

Remember, it's not what goes in, but what comes out that can have the greatest impact. Choose your words wisely.

It is when you criticize others, you need to understand that you are doing it out of your own fear, envy, insecurity, and lack of knowledge.

For if we had inner strength, confidence, faith, and understanding in all that we did, we would never utter another word of disdain to anyone. This can be a difficult lesson for most.

Your words have the ability
to manifest beautiful things
as well as destroy those
beautiful things.

"I am courageously open and embrace all experiences completely knowing that they are only learning experiences."

I Am Open

You came to Earth to learn and grow. Nothing more, nothing less.

When you are open to all experiences, you not only become more confident, you become fearless, knowing you can handle anything.

Know that when you stop thinking that you have to get everything right, you actually begin to discover who you are and why you chose to come here.

Remember, in order to teach, you must learn. And the best way to LEARN is through life EXPERIENCE.

We can have all the degrees and diplomas, but if we don't have any experience, then they are just pieces of paper that will become dust with time.

You are not here to teach others
until you have learned yourself.
Then and only then, can you teach.

"I release any anxiety, worry, or fear with regards to my life for I know that everything is working out perfectly."

I Am On Course

Take a look at your life and how it has unfolded up until now.

Look at every SUCCESS and how you got there.

Look at every CHALLENGE and how you overcame it.

Look at every DREAM you had and how it came true.

Because, if you really look, you will see that everything worked out just as it was supposed to.

Nothing happens by chance. Nothing at all. The only reason we run into problems is because we choose to stand in the way. Everything is working out for the greater good. Always.

You are going to be fine today,
and the next day, and
the day after that.

"The Presence of Spirit is revealed to me in a way I clearly understand through music, signs, people, feelings, and thoughts."

I Am Presence

Get to know the Presence within you and around you. Spirit will guide you in every way. Always.

All you have to do is to talk to Your Presence, God, Creator, as I am talking to you. Authentically.

When you need a sign, make sure you pay attention to all that is around you, for it can be as simple as a few words on a billboard or a song that you hear.

Know this: When you are genuine and humble in your search for knowledge, that is when you will discover that you knew it all along.

We have an amazing supernatural guidance that has ALWAYS been with us. And that guidance will never lead us astray…EVER.

You know in your heart
that you are not alone.
You never have been.

"I let no one tell me what I am
capable and not capable
of accomplishing.
I know I am successful in my
own right because I CAN."

I Am Capability

If someone tells you that you can't…and you believe them, then they are RIGHT.

If someone tells you that you shouldn't…and you believe them, then they are RIGHT.

If someone tells you that you won't…and you believe them, then they are RIGHT.

So who are "they" anyway and what "RIGHT" do they have to tell you anything?

Next time, tell "they" that they are WRONG.

Right now, let's tell ourselves that we CAN. Speak these words: "I WILL because I CAN."

Don't be surprised that when you
start thinking for yourself,
many will run away from you.

"I choose only those people
and experiences that will
help me not only become
a successful person, but
a better human."

I Am Selective

What's important to you?
Who's important to you?

Are you choosing the right people and experiences that will get you to where you want to be and most of all, stay with you through the long haul no matter what?

Are you being true to yourself? Are you being true to others? Are you being true to your life?

You have a choice to do EVERYTHING and ANYTHING. If you make the wrong choice…then make a new one. It's that simple. Think about that before you choose.

Remember, we are only as strong or weak as the company we keep. Our inner circle has just as much power to either help us succeed or fail.

You have a choice.
You always have a choice
to choose what you want.
Stop thinking otherwise.

"The dreams I have are manifesting now because I think about them constantly in a positive and imaginative way."

I Am Imagination

The dreams that you have inside of you, are closer to becoming a reality than you think.

When you dream within your imagination, you are actually creating a new reality. Keep replaying that reality and eventually it will come true.

Don't stop the process by disbelief. If you can imagine it, then it was meant to happen. Why would it not? It came into your thoughts. Did it not?

Know this: We are constantly creating dreams with our thoughts. Those fleeting moments of imagination are actually what is deep within our subconscious, reminding us of what we have forgotten. Don't make light of those thoughts for they hold messages of the future.

You need to start believing that
dreams are more real than the reality
that you believe to be real.

"I live each day to its fullest,
no matter where I am or what
I am doing, knowing that the
more I live in the present,
the more I create."

I Am Present

What have you done with this precious gift you were given called…Life?

Live each day to the fullest, no matter where you are or what you have. For when you live your best, you become your best.

Live in the PRESENT.

Focus on the FUTURE.

Release the PAST.

When you focus on the past only, you stay in the past. When you focus on the future only, you are relying on what is not yet.

When we stay in TODAY, we are creating our TOMORROW. Feel healthy today, feel wealthy today, feel joyful today.

You have the power to create
any future you desire
by staying in the present.

"I write my story from the depths of my heart, knowing that if I am authentic and honest, God helps me create the life I so desire."

I Am Author

I don't know what to do…I don't know how to do…
I don't know when to do…I don't know why to
do…I don't know where to do…

Any more excuses you would like to add as to why
you are not living the life you truly desire?

Go back to The Preface (The Story) on page ix and
rewrite from your heart, then really look at it. Thank
God in advance for helping you find your way.

Still confused? Ask yourself this: What house do I
want? What career do I want? Where would I want to
live? Should I marry or not? Should I have kids or not?

What would I want to do every day that would give
me joy?

We write our own story from our own heart, our own source.

You have all the answers
you need within you.
All you have to do is ask.

"I attract people with the
positive qualities
that I desire."

I Am Attraction

Know this: If you believe people are out to get you…then you will attract exactly those people.

If you believe people are no good, lazy, rude, mean or selfish…Then guess what?

You will attract those people into your life. Start now, by thinking of the kinds of relationships you want in your life. Go silently into your imagination and think of the people you want to start attracting into your life now. It is that easy.

But keep in mind, we must possess the same qualities that we desire in others. It is those relationships that we attract because of what we have become.

You have the power to create
the life you want by focusing
only on what you want.

"I live a powerful life because I choose to speak only powerful words."

I Am Word

If you truly want to change your life, there is but one powerful way to do so that will produce miraculous results and that is; CONTROL YOUR WORDS.

Speak only to that which you desire to be created in your life. It has been said that what comes out of your mouth is more important that what goes in.

Try for one day to speak little. Only say what is very important and to the point. See how others respond.

Know this: When we speak fewer words, we create more powerful energy that allows us to change all that we desire.

You become what you say.

"I remove the chains of mediocrity and break free to spread my wings and fly above the mountains of greatness."

I Am Greatness

Take a look at your life right now. How bad is it? Not that bad you say? Then why are you still doing the same thing you've been doing?

Why are you still doing the same thing you've been doing day after day, year after year?

I'll tell you why…because it's safe. Safety equals confinement, which always keeps you trapped in a never-ending cycle of boredom and mediocrity.

Think of one thing that you have always wanted to do, yet were afraid or unsure of. Think about it all day. THEN GO DO IT!

It is time that we break the chains and fly free. Then, and only then, will life be grand.

You need to take a risk today.
Do not delay. Go now.
Do something you have
always wanted to do.

"I am a risk-taker because I know I have the courage to experience life like never before."

I Am Courage

There are no guarantees in life. If there were, there would be no miracles whatsoever.

Guarantees allow you to play it safe. When you play it safe, you miss out on what could have been.

If you are waiting for a safety net before you leap, then you might as well stay home and wait…for the rest of your life.

What is holding you back? What would happen if you were to let go of the very thing that is holding you back? That is something you should be thinking about often.

When we refuse to step outside the box, we remain cornered and trapped.

You must ignore others
who are fearful and disrespectful
of your inner strength.

"I am successful beyond what
many could only imagine
because I have become
exceptionally GREAT
at one thing."

I Am Specific

K now this: In order to be truly successful, you must become exceptionally GREAT at ONE thing and less proficient at SEVERAL things.

Everyone has a gift or talent that deems them as a prodigy. However, you must discover this gift or talent by searching deep within your heart.

What are you good at? What would you love to do all day and every day? And what if you were asked to do it for free?

If you can answer that…then you have just discovered your perfect vocation.

Now imagine your life once you have found your special gift…

We must go out and become the BEST at what we do BEST. Stay focused. Stay determined and persistent. Put everything into it.

You are the gift that is awaiting inside of you.
Look within and you will discover gold.

"I get a second chance every day to start fresh with a clean slate, free from yesterday."

I Am Anew

You get a "DO-OVER" every time you wake up. So get up, wipe the slate clean and get on with it.

Yesterday is gone. Quit dragging it around with you like unwanted mud on your shoe.

Know this: The past that you think is a part of you, is actually "Dust in the Wind" and is no longer a part of your reality as you believe it to be.

When you wake every morning, repeat;

"I speak health, wealth, joy, peace, fulfillment and blessings to this day. All day. Thank you."

We are a NEW person every day. Our mind is a NEW mind every day.

You are brand new today.
How will you use this profound
knowledge right now?

"I forgive myself for
not seeing the sameness
in others that I see in me.
I thank those who have
shown me different."

I Am Sameness

The person you are refusing or struggling to forgive… is the one you need to forgive the most. Why?

Because you are exactly like them. They are you and you are they. You possess that same undesirable quality in them that you are unable to forgive.

It's time to forgive them and yourself. Remember, when we refuse to forgive, we become ill within.

Forgiveness opens more doors to opportunity more than anything else. Once you forgive, the whole world becomes yours.

Forgive and forget, for only then will we have the power to have, be, or do ANYTHING we desire.

You are the forgiveness in others
that is needed for yourself.

"I am the only one
living my life by making
my own choices based
on how I choose
to live."

I Am Choice

Where does it say that you have to play by the rules? You may have to abide by the laws, but no one said anything about the rules.

The most successful people in this world stepped out of the line, detaching themselves from the crowd to start their own path.

Stop thinking you have to be, act or do what others do in order to be successful in life.

Be wild. Be different. Be risky. Be over the top. Be adventurous. Be strange. Be YOU.

We were created to be UNIQUE. By remaining the SAME, each of us becomes like EVERYONE else.

You are like no one else.
Your life is like no other.
Free yourself now by being you,
and only you.

"I see my emotions for
what they are...
'Sign Posts' telling me I am
going in that direction."

I Am Direction

Yes, you are allowed to feel sorry for yourself. Yes, you are allowed to feel defeated. Yes, you are allowed to feel life isn't fair. Why?

Because you are human. You are allowed to feel and embrace any emotion. But when you let corrosive emotions define you, that's when you become emotionally unstable.

Emotions give you the ability to look closely at your life. If you are unhappy, then you are not creating correctly.

Start thinking about what makes you happy. Keep thinking about those happy moments and allow them to redirect your disposition.

When we begin to FEEL happiness, the universe will send more experiences to reinforce even more happiness.

You must think only happy thoughts
to create happy experiences.

"I am the mirror of change,
for when I experience
any undesirable trait from
another, I understand that
I am reflecting myself."

I Am Reflection

The conflicts that you are having with others are only mirrors reflecting back at you.

Change yourself and the mirrors will change.

Every person in your life is reflecting back a part of you that needs to be acknowledged in order for you to understand what needs to change about you.

It's a hard pill to swallow, but you must realize that everything around you is only mirrors, reflecting back an illusion that you created.

If we want to know the TRUTH, we must look deep within the mirror of life to SEE.

You have all the power in the
world to change what you see
that is right in front of you.

"The life I am living is shaped by Divine guidance from God in a way that I am open to receiving and understanding."

I Am Understanding

The time you are wasting cannot be returned. The time is now to live how you have always wanted to. Not sure how? Just ask.

The Presence within will show you the dream and purpose of your heart. But you must open your eyes and ears for any signs that will lead the way.

Be silent. Be still. Be in the natural. Be open and authentic in your search. Then you will be found.

It's not a matter of believing in something greater than ourselves; it's about believing that we are great. When we do this, we get back the power we've always had.

You are the presence within
and you have all the knowledge
needed to do what you need to do.

"I am grateful for everything in my life now. I say thank you when I need help, healing and guidance. I say thank you to create change now."

I Am Gratitude

Be grateful for what you have now…even if it's not much.

The more you say "Thank You" NOW, the more you will receive NOW.

When you are grateful and say "Thank You" for all you have now, you will receive more…effortlessly.

Every time you say thank you, the universe takes note and makes sure that you receive your due before anyone else. When you let God know that you are grateful for EVERYTHING NOW, abundant blessings will be sent.

Saying THANK YOU is the ultimate expression that will create all we desire instantly. Always and forever.

You only need to know two words
that will give you the power
to have whatever you want:
Thank You.

"The mountain I see in front of me isn't real, for I know it is only an illusion within my mind."

I Am Defiant

Every one of you has faced an obstacle to overcome, or mountain to climb. Some face one every day.

But it is those that believe the mountain isn't real, who climb effortlessly to the top. Every time.

What if I told you that everything you see in your world isn't real, including you? Just illusions. How would you live your life then?

Know this: Nothing in your reality is real, until you make it real, by saying it is so. Stop listening to what others believe is real. Just because someone says it is so…doesn't make it so for you.

We have all stood at the base of what seemed like mountain too big to climb. It's time for us to climb the mountain. Move the mountain. Tackle the mountain. Accept the mountain. Level the mountain. Make friends with the mountain.

You are the mountain that is in your way.
You are the only one that can
remove that mountain.

"I practice compassion by not judging or condemning others, or myself."

I Am Nonjudgmental

When you judge and condemn others for any reason, you are judging and condemning yourself. Your judgment of the other—without fail—comes back to you as judgment for yourself.

It is none of your business as to what others think, speak, feel, act or live for that matter. It only matters what you do. Stay focused only on yourself.

What is wrong for you, might be right for someone else. And the same goes for the other. What is right isn't necessarily wrong, nor what is wrong necessarily right. It is only your perspective.

When we become accusers, we are really accusing ourselves. Know this: Everything we put out in front of us, comes back in the like.

You need never condemn
or judge others, including
yourself first and foremost.

"I am a great leader because I am a great follower too, and I understand that there is no difference in either."

I Am Dutiful

Are you a leader or a follower? Because in truth, they are one in the same.

You must follow to lead and lead to follow. The greatest leaders and teachers are the ones that mastered how to follow and lead with humility, compassion and grace.

Great leaders bow down first. Great leaders will wash others' feet. Great leaders know the Law and the TRUTH. They allow their followers to be as such. Great leaders are those who free the mind, not imprison it.

If we have not mastered the ability to follow, then we are not able to lead. If we are unable to lead, it's because we have not learned how to follow.

You were designed to lead and follow.
Follow and lead. Lead and follow.
Follow and lead.

"I am flying free as a bird because I allow absolutely no one to attach strings to me or my life."

I Am Unrestrained

No one except yourself has any right to control or dictate the way you live or anything else for that matter.

If you continually let someone pull your strings, you will remain an unhappy puppet for the rest of your life.

Cut yourself loose and you will experience a freedom like never before. Be free. Be strong. Be fearless. Be adventurous. Be you no matter where you are or what you have been through.

We must realize that we live among a collective that for the most part are unaware of the power of intention. We all have this powerful law available to us.

You need nothng to be free.
You are already free
within your mind.

"Every day is a new adventure, a new experience and a new story because I am the author of my life. Whatever I put down on paper comes true in one way or another."

I Am Word

Life is but a journey. Reaching your destiny is never set in stone, for your story is ever-changing.

You are the author of your life. What story are you writing?

Create any story that you would love to live. Write it down. Create a vision board. Pretend and play make believe. Do this and I promise you, it will come true.

Right now, where you are, picture something you want. See it clear as day. Hold that thought for but a moment. Do this every day, and I promise you, it will manifest into your life. I have seen miracles happen for many by doing this simple exercise.

We can manifest ANYTHING just by thinking about it and most of all, FEELING IT.

You are the story of your life.
Period.

"I am provided for as long as I keep moving forward, even if it's one step at a time. I will always have what I need."

I Am Providence

Know this: God takes care of everyone, including you, as long as you make a conscious effort to keep going. Take one step every day and God will empower you with two steps. Promise.

No matter where you are in life, keep walking forward. Your Creator knows exactly what you need and want. Hold out your hand and God will hold you up.

Stand up, right now. Take one step forward. Hold out your hand. Soon you will feel a sense of peace wash over you, and then you will know that you are good.

Know this, we are NEVER without. The universe will always provide us with the abundance that continues in this world and beyond. The surplus is infinite.

You are never alone.
Once you realize this,
nothing can stop you.

"I stand for all that is good
in the world with courage,
honesty, and realism, even if
it means standing alone."

I Am Good

Always stand UP for the greater good. Always stand BEHIND the people you care about. Always stand FIRM on what you believe in. Always stand OUT because you are different. Always stand PROUDLY for you are capable. Always stand TALL knowing you are brave enough to do all the above.

We always stand up for what we know to be TRUTH, even if it goes against that which may seem right to others.

You are the good because you
believe in the good.

"I am focused and attentive to all the signs, symbols, and revelations God sends, guiding me successfully to my destiny."

I Am Destiny

There is an Intelligence that sits in the silence waiting to lead you to a life you never imagined.

Everything happens for a reason. Nothing is by chance. Pay attention to what is happening and then you will understand why it is happening. Stay focused on every detail of your life and beyond.

You must sit in silence with your eyes opened and forward. Pay attention to EVERYTHING. Do not discard anything just because you don't understand it.

When we acknowledge this Higher Guidance and are grateful for it, we will never, ever have to look for anything that we need or want, for it will manifest in one way or another.

You are the intelligence
that you seek. Start paying
attention to yourself.

"As I sit in the silence, surrounded only by Nature, I am open to the knowledge of Divine Intelligence."

I Am Natural

Unplug…right now.

Sit in silence surrounded by Nature—no man-made influence whatsoever around you. It is in this reality that you will hear and know the answers you seek. You are missing out on a world of magic when you are plugged in to technology.

Free yourself and you will experience Heaven here on Earth.

Remove yourself from the modern chaos that surrounds you. Only then, will you be given the answers you seek by utilizing all six senses at all times.

This may seem hard to do because technology has become so pervasive in the world today. But imagine what this can do.

Going outdoors and experiencing nature will reinvigorate and remind us of how we were meant to think and feel.

You are a species that thrives in nature. When you live in nature you become empowered.

"I have everything
I need right now and my
belief makes it so."

I Am Fulfilled

When you let go of your desperate need for any-thing…that is when everything will come to you effortlessly. Release your grip. Let go now. Neediness repels. Know that there is nothing you need that isn't already yours.

Just believe you have it now. Then get on with other things and it will appear.

We are CREATORS and MANIFESTORS. We have EVERY-THING we need at our fingertips, (actually our thoughts). When we think about what we want, it CAN drop right in front of us at the right time.

You are already what you
desire and need.

"I meet the rough terrain head-on with confidence, determination, and faith."

I Am Adaptation

Just because the road you're on now is rocky, it doesn't mean that you are heading to a rough destination. Just the opposite.

The easy road never leads you to satisfaction or abundance.

You chose this path because you knew you could master it.

Many stay safe on the shoulder and never go past the warning signs. That is why they are stuck.

Get behind the wheel. Ask God for a map and proper directions. And when we receive them, don't hesitate. Go forward with confidence and know that the road ahead is OURS for the taking.

You are going in the direction
you chose. You can change the road
and direction at any time.

"I await and pay close attention for Divine guidance because when I listen, look and understand, the signs are right in front of me."

I Am Opportunity

Your life is being Divinely guided with precision. So slow down and pay attention, for you might be missing out on many doors of abundant opportunities.

Start now, by sitting still in the quiet and ask for a sign. Any sign that you will understand. Then stay focused. It may take a while, but you will get a sign. Promise.

Turn OFF and put AWAY all man-made technology. Go outside and sit under a tree. Now ASK. Then be quiet until you get an answer.

We all have nonphysical guides, masters and teachers around us at all times, giving us direction, guidance and support. BE OPEN.

You are far from being alone.
Ask any question that you
desire an answer to.

"I am worthy of wealth and financial security because my thoughts and actions attract money, wealth, and abundance."

I Am Money

Your lack of money is a result of the current belief you have about money. Nothing more and nothing less.

Any negative thoughts, words or feelings about money will repel all money that is on its way to you.

Keep in mind: Money is not the goal.

Money is energy, just as with everything else, including you. The most important thing to consider here is, "Do you feel worthy of having money?"

As manifestors and creators, we don't need money to get EVERYTHING we want. All we have to do is THINK about it. THINK about it and WAIT for it to appear at the right time.

You are as wealthy as you see
and believe yourself to be.

"I am at peace right now even
though I know that what
I'm experiencing right
now will change."

I Am Change

What's it going to take for you to know and believe that you are going to be just fine?

Know this: Life is ever-changing and until you embrace ALL change, you will continue to resist it and continue to beat yourself down mercilessly.

Instead, believe that with every change, you are getting closer to the desire in one way or another.

You CAN and WILL make it. Why? Because YOU are the CHOSEN one, something you have forgotten.

No matter what is happening now...we will always prosper one way or another. The sooner we believe this, the sooner change will come.

You are going to be fine.
Because you have always been fine.

"I am doing what I love
every day knowing I will
experience and enjoy
a successful living."

I Am Talent

Work hard to live an easy life...RIGHT? Not necessarily. God gave you a talent, like everyone else. However, it is up to you to discover that talent, or gift if you will. So how does one go about this?

It's simple. Ask yourself what calls to your heart. What makes you feel alive and excited about life?

If you still find yourself in bewilderment, ask yourself this, "If money were not an issue, what would I love to do all day long for free?" When you come with an answer to this profound question, then you have found your gift, your talent.

Now, go research, study, and learn all you can to perfect and express your talent. Then your life will have purpose and meaning.

Our only purpose here on Earth is to peacefully express our inner truth. When we help others by expressing ourselves, we express love. Period.

You have what it takes to do what you love.
Waste no more time. Go now.

"I know what I want because
my Truth is in my heart,
not in my head."

I Am Movement

Sometimes life happens, and it takes you on a turbulent ride going nowhere. Despite all that, the Truth in your heart remains your foundation which will drive your life forward.

If you are constantly making choices without direction, something or someone else will make them for you.

Right now, you may think you know what you want. As your mind comes up with many ideas, ask yourself, "Why do I want this?" Unless your mind is following your heart, your mind will be spinning its wheels, getting you nowhere. On the other hand, by knowing and understanding your heart, your thoughts and actions will propel and reinforce that desire until it comes into your life. It's that SIMPLE.

We must stop looking for the answers in the mind. Look deep within the heart and listen, then go get it...now.

You are the only one that creates your life.
What are you creating?

"I can change any mirage that I see by walking towards it fearlessly as it fades away."

I Am Formless

When you fight against anything, you create negative resistance which creates more of what you are fighting against.

Instead, embrace it not as a threat, but only a mirage of your current reality.

Only then, will you be able to walk towards it with courage and confidence as it disappears.

Remember, what you see in front of you is NOTHING but an illusionary form that will dissipate upon your command at any time.

What we believe either becomes a friend or a foe. No one is an expert at anything. It Is us. We are the experts when we begin to remember who we are. We become FORM.

You must realize that nothing
you see is real. Only then can you
create something real.

"I now change myself
in order for others
to follow suit."

I Am Change

I t is not your spouse, boss, coworkers, friends, kids or neighbors that need to change.

It is YOU and only YOU.

When you change, the energy around you changes effortlessly. Become exactly who your heart knows you are, then others will resonate your energy and change as such.

If you find yourself surrounded by difficult people, you must look at you, yourself. Are you difficult?

Remember, we attract the like into our life, and this includes others. Most of those who come into our lives, are that of mirrors reflecting back at us. These mirrors remind us of something within that needs to be changed for our Higher Good.

Your life becomes exactly as you are.
Who are you?

"I know without a doubt that
I am perfect in every way,
just as God created me to be."

I Am Perfection

You were made in the image of your Creator...so you are already Perfect. IT IS TIME TO STOP FORGETTING THAT.

In the eyes of our Creator, you are perfect. When you believe different, that is when there is contradiction.

Know that if you are feeling out of place or very different than others, it means that you have been chosen for a Higher Calling. So be it.

When we understand that we were meant to be healthy, prosperous, joyful, and fulfilled, we understand the knowledge that states, "We are already perfect and flawless in every way."

You become less of your perfect self
when you forget who you are.

"I am surrounded by love, knowing I will have many opportunities to experience a special love...at the right time."

I Am Experience

L ove is never lost or gone. It just transitions. If you could truly understand and embrace this, there would be no more broken hearts.

Those who FALL out of love, struggle to understand what TRUE love is or what it can ever be because they don't know who they are yet, or who they ever were to begin with.

Know this: Most people tend to perceive love in SUPERFICIAL ways that are not real at all. Love is deeper than anything one could ever comprehend. When you realize this, you will never fall out of love, just transition in to it.

If we could just hold on through this transition, we would experience a love like never before.

You are love as it is. When you understand this, you need not look for it anymore.

"Money flows easily and effortlessly to me because I have no need to desperately chase it down."

I Am Attraction

I t is not that people earn money. It's that they attract it with their thoughts and beliefs.

Money has to be attracted to you. If you are fearful of it, desperate for it, or chase after it…money will inevitably RUN AWAY.

Know this: Money is just energy. And energy is neither created nor destroyed. It just changes into something different. It's not money you need; it's the energy to create what you truly want.

The most important thing we need to consider when it comes to money or prosperity of any kind, is that we MUST feel WORTHY of having it to begin with. If we don't feel we deserve money, then we will never partake of any.

You are money and
money is you.

"I cherish all that comes in and goes out of my life without the need to hold onto anything tightly for fear of losing it."

I Am Release

You must never hold onto anything too tightly, because in "truth" it was never yours to keep in the first place.

It is only an experience to cherish along your journey. When you fear losing something or someone, it creates negative energy, which in turn, repels that very thing or person.

We need to mentally let go of all that is in our life now. When we sit in the silence of our aloneness, it is there we discover that we have all that we need, right there. All of the rest, is extra.

You come into this world alone,
and you leave this world alone.
But are you really alone?

"I am making the right decision promptly, for I know God is guiding my every step."

I Am Decision

Make a decision and make it now. The more time you hesitate, the more you will create static that blocks the flow of abundant energy.

If you are truly unsure as to what you want to do, try this:

Place each possibility in writing. The one that pulls at your heart is the thing that you desire. Do not let your head decide otherwise.

Then sit still in the quiet. Ask the Presence to help you with that decision—as with ALL decisions—and then wait, knowing you have already been answered.

When we are indecisive, we are telling the world we don't have a clue as to who we are or what we want. This creates failure on all levels.

Your heart already knows exactly
what you want. It just needs to
convince your head.

"I am a master at creating anything I desire because I think, speak, feel, and act as if I already have what I desire."

I Am Vision

Here's how to manifest anything you want.
Think about it as if it has already manifested.
Speak about it as if it has already manifested.
Feel about it as if it has already manifested.
Act like it has already manifested.

Create a vision board with images, symbols, and words that reflect the desire you would like to manifest in your life. Don't be shy.

It's been said that 90% of all vision boards come true. The other 10% is already here.

There is nothing that you can't have. And guess what? You don't necessarily have to work hard for it. Actually you NEVER do. It will just drop in your lap if you allow yourself to receive it.

We are all cocreators with the universe, sparked by our limitless imagination.

If you can't see it,
you can't become it.

"I fully embrace every feeling I experience with strength, love, and trust knowing that suppressing them will only create imbalance on all levels."

I Am Human

The pain in your heart is warranted. It reminds you that you are human. Embrace your pain completely. Feel it with every fiber of your being for as long as you need. This is true healing.

When you hide, block out or ignore your feelings, you are literally poisoning your body and environment.

Know this: Feelings are very different from emotions. Feelings come from the heart. Emotions come from the head. If you try to rationalize how you feel, you inevitably become emotional.

We need to embrace our humanness. That is why we chose to come here to this physical place we call Earth. Completely feel and experience ALL that we can.

You are human.
Don't forget that.

"I attract people who are supportive of my success."

I Am Selection

If you truly want to be a success beyond all that you could ever imagine, you need to have people close to you who are 100% on board with you.

If not, you need to distance yourself so that you can soar to great heights. Those who have achieved great success, had a small inner circle of people and refused to let anything or anyone negative come into that circle.

Know this: If we let negative influences into not only our circles, but our lives, they will eventually wreak havoc and continually cause us to pick up after them.

Your innermost circle of people will either help you succeed or help you fail.

"I move forward with confidence knowing that what I truly want and what is truly important to me will ultimately define who I AM."

I Am Definition

If you stand around hesitating, the Universe will pull the rug out from where you are standing…every time.

Many wonder why they find their lives upside down all of a sudden. It's because they lost sight of what they want or who they are.

If they overlook or forget the definition of themselves and/or their desires, life will appear blurred and vague.

Know that you have all it a takes to go after what you want. Do not look at what is in front of you now. You must look beyond your reality to see what it is you want.

The universe will turn the world upside down if we get too comfortable in life. We are chosen to uphold the definition of ourselves—the light. We can't do it by just feeling comfortable all of the time.

You need to stop letting other
people, experiences, or circumstances
dictate your life.

"I experience oneness when
I see everyone as a brilliant,
bright light, including myself."

I Am All

If you are experiencing conflict with others or dealing with difficult people…imagine them as brilliant, bright lights and I promise you they will change right before your eyes.

Those who come into your life are there to remind you of what kind of person you want to become or what kind of person you don't want to become, thus ultimately letting you know what kind of person you have become.

Take a good look at those around you. What do you see? Them? You? Both?

When we see everyone as one, we realize everyone is…one.

You become the person
you choose by emulating those
you see as your true self.

"I hold my dreams sacred, sharing them only with those I trust, for I understand that negative energy from others can have a negative effect on my dreams."

I Am Sacred

Don't tell your dreams to just anyone, including those who aren't in support of you or sharing your vision. Period.

Dreams that are in your heart are sacred. They come from a place many fear. It is those that will share their fear when you share your dream.

Human nature has shown, there are people—including those close to you—who don't really want you to succeed, for that would cause inferiority or envy for the most part. It reminds them of what they are afraid of and why they are still stuck in the same place.

Our dreams are what make us come ALIVE. If we share them with the wrong people, we will find ourselves and our dreams DEAD to the world.

You are only the dreams that arc inside
of you. It is when you become those
dreams that you become real.

"I maintain my garden today, so that I may prosper tomorrow by planting and nurturing only positive seeds and removing negative weeds."

I Am Seed

In many ways, a seed is like a thought, word, feeling, and action. On its own, a seed does not grow. When planted and cared for, amazing things happen.

A desire is a seed (positive thought) that you plant in life's garden. Every garden needs to be tended to by removing the weeds (negative thoughts). Water it with positive thoughts and wait patiently for it to grow.

Know that what you are doing TODAY is planting seeds for TOMORROW, and the growth you are experiencing now, is from the seeds you planted YESTERDAY. Are they weeds? Or beautiful flowers?

It is when we think, speak, and act only as to what it is we desire to manifest, does our garden become that of Eden.

You are the only one that is tending to the garden of life. Are you planting for a healthy life or useless weeds?

"I am humbly open and embrace all change knowing that it will come to pass before I know it to be."

I Am Open-Minded

Know this…Nothing remains the same forever. Change is inevitable…Always.

What you are going through will eventually pass. I promise.

By remaining humble and open-minded every day with a positive attitude, the change you seek will come sooner rather than later. Always.

Once you understand that nothing is real until you make it real, then and only then are you able to embrace the nothingness that comes before all change.

Keep in mind, when change happens, especially abrupt and even painful change, it means that we are on the cusp of something great. Just Keep Going.

You are the only change that you seek.

"I remain compassionate and patient as I accept others as they are, knowing they are learning as I."

I Am Patience

You are living your life the best way you know how. And you are doing this among others who are doing the same.

Life is nothing but a class room and there are many people learning on different levels.

The people around you may not have the same thoughts or opinions as you. Be open to everything that is presented to you, for you just might learn something that you would have resisted because of your defensiveness.

When we truly understand the power of patience, compassion will be the only thing we feel.

You become that which is an enigma
you see in others.

"I am worth $_____"

(Fill in the blank and begin to believe without any doubt that you are worth that much.)

I Am Worth

How much are you worth? Really think about this because the Universe will pay any price.

A penny?

A dollar?

A million?

Know this…I have witnessed several people become millionaires because they believed they were millionaires already.

Money is not what you think it is. It's not something just to pay the bills with. Money is energy that you can shape, mold, enjoy, or help others with. What most people don't realize is that you can manifest ALL the things you desire WITHOUT money. I promise you that. This is TRUTH.

If we base our self-worth on what we think we are worth… unlimited prosperity is just a thought away.

You are only as rich as you
believe you are worth.

"I experience Heaven any time
I choose, for I know God is not
forsaking me. It is only I,
who believes different."

I Am Heaven

The only hell that exists is in your mind. Cleanse, heal and rebuild your mind and then you will experience Heaven right here.

Start by acknowledging that you have a choice, to either think lower level thoughts or higher level thoughts.

God is not the one punishing you. It is you, and only you, who is punishing yourself. I struggled with this mindset for years, assuming I was cursed or in purgatory. But I realized that wasn't so and knew to keep my eye on the GOOD…which includes me as well.

We are not victims, so stop acting like it. Each one of us is a cocreator. Get up. Ask the universe to be our cocreator partner and start building a new life today.

You can see heaven right
now by thinking about it.

"My belief that anything is possible makes it attainable."

I Am Possiblitiy

Your doubt is preventing you from seeing the possible. When you doubt, you are saying that there is only one way, thus leading you astray from the right path.

Doubt becomes your nemesis. Everyone has an infinite intelligence within them that communicates all that is needed to know in order to fully navigate life successfully. Be quiet, be still and LISTEN.

It is when you remove doubt completely from your existence that you will you have the ability to become what you were truly meant to be.

Know this: We doubt most of the time because we are basing thoughts on what others think and believe. Stop right now and go within to where the only real answers are.

You are more confident then
you could ever imagine.

"I experience all I desire at any time by believing and being authentic."

I Am Authenticity

I t's not a matter of being a "good" person in order to receive what you desire. It's only a matter of believing that you will receive what you desire.

When you try to manipulate, you become superficial, thus sending a clear signal that you are willing to acquire through deceptive measures.

Know that you have everything you need right now. You just need to ask for it with an authentic humility. Then wait for it to appear at the right time.

Remember, you can create ANYTHING out of thin air, which is energy, as EVERYTHING is. Intend to manifest all that you need. This is your God-given ability.

When we are humbly authentic, we inherit more than just the Earth.

You can have whatever you want
at any time. Always.

"I am living an abundant life now that my actions reflect my intentions without fail."

I Am Sustainable

I t's never too late for anything. For there is no time and space in "truth." It is humans who believe they must conform to clocks and calendars.

Truth be told, most discover their success after the age of 55 or older. And that success generates a greater return now than it would have in their early years.

What is it you love to do? ("I don't know" is not an answer.) Look deep within your heart and you will discover the very thing that will bring you much joy and success.

The best way to determine as to what will make us a success? Figure out what we love to do if money were not an issue.

Your time is now. Go be who
you were destined to be.

"My success is here and now because I am strong enough to take on every test, obstacle and adversary that comes my way."

I Am Challenge

The world and beyond will test you to the core just to see if you will fail or give up. But only when you pass every test, do you succeed and surpass all adversity without fail.

Remember, you created your adversity so that you wouldn't forget how strong you are. You have it around to keep you from getting too comfortable and lazy.

Don't stop. Don't look back. Keep moving forward with sheer determination and GUTS.

The obstacles, difficulties and challenges we begin to experience just means we are closer to success.

Adversity is your grandest
test for a reason.

"I am what I choose to receive. Therefore, I manifest everything into my life on purpose and not by default."

I Am A Boomerang

What you put out into the world and beyond is what you will always get back in return. What are you putting out there?

Success?	Happiness?
Gratitude?	Love?
Peace?	Compassion?

Or

Poverty?	Hate?
Blame?	Disdain?
Complaining?	Illness?

Know this: What you are thinking, speaking and feeling is creating your reality right now. You and only YOU are attracting EVERYTHING that you are experiencing right now.

This is very important. Life doesn't just happen to us. We created every aspect of the life we are living right now. We are also creating every aspect of the life we will be living.

You receive exactly what you send out.

"I make choices that are beneficial to my health, wealth and fulfillment in this life knowing that I am solely responsible for making those choices in the first place."

I Am Choice

There are no mistakes, just choices. If you make a choice you don't like…make another one.

Many say they don't have a choice. And I say they're wrong.

You have a choice to believe you have a choice. That is your very first step to changing your life.

You can choose to be happy…

You can choose to be healthy…

You can choose to be successful…

You can choose to live life…

You can choose…

We must understand that in life there will always be choices to be made. And how we make those choices is from the knowledge that we obtain to do so. Ask God for guidance before making those choices…I promise it will make all the difference.

You are the chosen. How will you choose to use this knowledge?

"I stand fearless knowing that when faced with the unknown, it is only an illusion that hasn't been completely formed yet by me."

I Am Fearless

The fear you are feeling is real because you have made it real. Embrace it completely, right now. Then let go of it.

What are you afraid of? Really?

Think about that. What's the worst that can happen? Change? Success?

Fear is the most devastating emotion. I have seen many lives wasted due to the emotion of fear.

Fear is nothing but your mind telling your body that you CAN'T.

Go Now. Do something that scares you.

When we eliminate the fear, we create a strength that is unstoppable.

You are the fear that is keeping you in a nightmare of your own making.

"I put forth my best effort knowing that every masterpiece was created with vision, focus, and persistence."

I Am A Masterpiece

If you do lazy work…you get lazy results.

Everything you do should come from your best. Everything.

If you try to cut corners, the Universe can do the same.

I am not talking about hard physical work. Not even. I am talking about putting your whole self into everything that matters only to you.

Stop giving "half" the effort with everything you do…everything that is of substance took time…a lot of time.

When we give everything our best, we create the best. Always.

If you don't love what you do, you will
never make it work, no matter
how hard you try.

"I release the door that is closed and embrace the new door that is open, for I know I am the one who created both."

I Am Closure

Stop knocking on the door that just closed and pay attention to the door that's opening right now.

Whatever door that is closing, was meant to close, for you are the one who actually closed it.

You must understand that when you grasp the past tightly, you are suffocating your future.

Release your grip and the flow of certainty will grace your mind with a new opportunity.

Walk away from the closed door and look for the one that is opening. Walk through it with confidence.

There is nothing that we need right here and now that we don't already have.

You have the key to open any door
in front of you. Stop sneaking
in through the back.

"I know now that the perfect
day for me is attainable,
just as is the perfect life."

I Am Attainment

If you were given a perfect day to live as you wish… how would that day look? Really think about this. Got it? Good

Now go live that life…right now. The only limitations that are holding you back, are the ones in your mind.

Start by imagining the life you wish to have EVERY day. I promise you it will become real. Don't let anything come between your thoughts. You must be vigilant and stay focused.

Know this: The world and everything in it was created by thought and thought alone.

Remember, we create our tomorrows with our thoughts today…right now.

Your life is only as good as your thoughts. Your thoughts are only as good as your imagination.

"I live my life as I want it to be by doing the work that needs to be done."

I Am Doing

You want to be HEALTHY but you refuse to take care of yourself.

You want to be RICH but you refuse to do the mental work.

You want to be LOVED but you refuse to open up your heart.

You want to be SUCCESSFUL but you refuse to take the risk.

I am not talking about action. I am talking about thinking. Start thinking about ONLY what you want to transpire into your life. Speak only what you want to happen in your life. Feel only what you desire.

Believing that we can obtain something by merely wishing, without affirming and doing the inner work, will always lead to failure.

You only resist what you don't understand.
Therefore you ignore what is.

"I am the only one that needs to believe in me. Therefore, I need validation only from within."

I Am Validation

I f you don't believe in yourself…
Then who will? Not they or them.

You never need others to validate who you are, or your talents or your worth for that matter. Because if you do, you'll be sitting around waiting forever, wasting precious time, just as they are.

When you base your worth on what others think or speak of you, you are playing a dangerous game that will inevitably lead to your demise.

Our self-worth is based on one thing, and one thing only… the TRUTH we hold within. Do not let ANYONE else deny that TRUTH.

You only need to validate your worth just
as your creator already has.

"I am successful no matter what because I understand that failure doesn't mean to give up. It means to get up and try again."

I Am Resilience

Failing is a good thing. It means you are actually trying.

Know that if you don't try, you have already failed. The most successful people have failed countless times before they got it right.

Keep trying, and trying, and trying, and trying, and trying and you will…get it right.

Know this: If you are failing to achieve what you truly desire in your heart, then your failing will not happen in vain.

When we fail, we are still putting ourselves forward, inch by inch, towards that which we see as success. Keep going and you will grab hold of it….WITHOUT FAIL.

You can only fail as often as you
think that you are failing.

"I control my thoughts in order to pave the way for miraculous change."

I Am Design

How can you create a life you desire, exactly as you want, within a very short period of time?

By RAISING your ENERGY. How do you do this? By constantly THINKING about what you want to come into your life. Think about who you want to become. Think about the life you have always wanted. Think about that often

The entire world was created by THOUGHT, and THOUGHT alone.

With a firm grip on our thoughts, we will create anything we desire. When we believe that, the Presence will adhere to our THOUGHTS.

You and your life become what
you think and feel. Period.

"There is happiness in my present reality, right where I am standing."

I Am Satisfied

Basing your happiness on looking forward only to something else in the future will leave you constantly yearning for more in the future.

Instead, be happy now in this moment, even if it is fleeting. No matter what is happening in your life or who you are right now, be joyful and know that the present is in the Presence and you need not look any further.

Know this: When you are happy no matter where you are, no matter what you are doing, no matter what the future holds or doesn't, you will manifest happiness…effortlessly.

We must enjoy and find favor in some aspect of the present for our lives to change into what we desire. Stay in the NOW.

You are creating your future right here
and now in the present.

"I am humble at all times
knowing that I am attracting
and receiving everything
that is good."

I Am Humility

Your ego will land you flat on your face…Every time. Living by ego makes you mentally and physically exhausted. If you are worn out by life itself, then you are living by your EGO.

It is when you let ego and pride take over that you find yourself at the bottom looking up wondering why nothing in your life is working.

You cannot destroy EGO. You can only subdue it, for it is needed as well. The temptation to follow your ego may be strong, but your determination and will are stronger.

When we remain consistently humble, we find ourselves able to navigate life with ease because the world becomes effortlessly ours.

You will live in constant paradise
when you live in constant humility.

"I am at peace within,
creating a peaceful energy
that resonates with the world."

I Am Calm

When you remain at peace at all times, with every situation, circumstance or experience, you create conditions that welcome the goodness of life. ...Every time.

It is when you fight and resist, that you block your prayers and miracles, because you actually draw yourself nearer, the very thing you are resisting.

Look at every situation, experience, circumstance and condition as neither bad nor good; then and only then, will it become as you desire it to be.

It is in that moment when we feel at peace with EVERYTHING as IT IS. That's when we become peaceful with ALL, including ourselves.

Your peaceful energy has a
ripple effect upon the world.

"My body is healing in many ways because I am healing my thoughts, words and attitude about life and myself."

I Am Wellness

When you experience illness or imbalance within your body, you are being asked to learn something about yourself. It is your illness that is making you well again.

Know this: ALL illness and disease is a result of your whole being…your mind, body, and spirit.

Your first step to wellness is to look at your thoughts about everything in your life, including you.

If we are holding on to any resentment, anger, fear, refusing to forgive, or wishing ill will for any reason, we are literally poisoning our bodies right now.

Your first step to getting well
and healing is to forgive yourself
for not being your true self.

"By knowing specifically what I want, I am in the process of manifesting every desire right now."

I Am Manifestation

To bring about change, you must reprogram your subconscious mind by repeating your desire or what you want changed, over and over, every day until it manifests.

Think, speak, feel and act as if what you desire has already come to pass. This is a power that everyone possesses, but most aren't sure of how to use it.

YOU MUST DO THE WORK.

If you are unsure as to who you are, what you want, and where you want to go…

Then ask the Presence every day to help you listen to your heart.

Remember, life doesn't just happen! We CREATE IT through manifestation.

God knows who you truly are.
It's up to you to experience the joy.

"Where I am today is a result of what I thought and did yesterday."

I Am Present

What you did in your past has created your present. What you are doing in your present is creating your future.

What are you CREATING right now?

This is crucial. Use every minute of every day to create a prosperous, joyful and fulfilling life, now and tomorrow. Don't waste any more time.

Forgive and release the PAST.

Plan and create in the PRESENT.

Believe in the FUTURE...NOW.

Know this: The less baggage from our past that we carry around, the more freedom we have to go about the present and future as we decide.

You must understand that there is only this moment. This very moment.

"All my relationships are based on truth and wholeness because I am complete as I AM."

I Am Complete

You do not need anyone else to be whole. You are already whole.

People who come together want to share their wholeness with each other.

If you are lonely and feel lost without another, then it is not a relationship you are looking for…it is YOUR "Self" within the Presence that you seek.

This is the "real" relationship.

If you find yourself unable to be alone with yourself, then you need to look within yourself to discover as to why you are running from yourself.

When we are complete and need absolutely nothing from others, that is when we are ready for a relationship.

Your relationship with yourself
will never leave you.

"I am getting better and better every day because I do one thing, no matter how small, to improve myself and create a better me."

I Am Improvement

Every day do one thing, no matter how big or small, that will improve YOU.

When you improve yourself, you attract…

Money

Health

Relationships

Opportunities

Remember, if you remain the same…Your life remains the same.

Be authentically **DIFFERENT** and dare to step away from the idiotic normalcy that plagues the world.

We must relentlessly strive to improve ourselves, for it will create the life we want.

You are a work-in-progress, learning and growing every day.

"I think only thoughts that I want to manifest into my life, knowing that my thinking is creating all that is around me."

I Am Thought

I t's not that you are getting OLD…It's that you have OLD thoughts.

It's not that you are UNHEALTHY…It's that you have UNHEALTHY thoughts.

It's not that you are BROKE…It's that you have POVERTY thoughts.

Think health, even if you are not.

Think wealth, even if you are not.

Think youth, even if you are not.

Think success, even if you are not.

Think possibility, even if there is none, and you will become what you think.

It's time that we dare to think beyond any limits that attempt to restrain our creative power.

When you think...you are.

"I am grateful for the ability to experience love, no matter the duration."

I Am Connection

Every relationship has a certain time frame. Some are short and some are long. And it is when you learn to accept this, you will be able to love unconditionally without need of any kind.

If you truly want a relationship with substance, then you must first have a relationship with yourself and the Presence. When you can feel secure in that, then and only then, will you be ready to take on other relationships.

Know this: It is only yourself that you truly need. Because the SELF is everything that IS.

God meant for relationships to be experiences, nothing more, nothing less. And it is what we do with those experiences that helps our souls to grow further.

You manifest all relationships
because they are you.

"My life is overflowing
with Abundance."

I Am Abundance

The page you have just opened contains a simple, yet powerful secret to living an abundant life and creating all that you desire.

No matter what your life is like now...Say "thank you" for everything that you have and everything you don't have.

Start by praising it and thanking it...NOW.

Do this every day...OFTEN and you will be GIVEN more abundant things to replace what you are already grateful for.

This secret is understood by many, yet practiced by few. When you let the Presence know that you are grateful for everything that you've received, and will receive...more will be GIVEN.

The most sacred secret known throughout the world about abundance: Be GRATEFUL and PRAISE the life we have NOW.

Thank you. Thank you. Thank you. Thank you.

"I surround myself with positive words, thoughts and actions TODAY."

I Am Positivity

Negative = poverty
Positive = wealth

When you are negative in any way, shape or form, you block all abundance that could be yours.

But if you are positive, you become rich beyond all that could be imagined.

Practice this for one day and see what happens.

Go and sit among the silence in nature. Sit with the Presence and ask to be shown what life would be like if you were to practice positivity.

Remember, the hell that we believe we are in, is the same place that we believe Heaven to be...the MIND.

In every aspect of life,
the positive mind will succeed.

"I remain confident, composed
and compassionate during all
interactions with others."

I Am Mastery

There is never a need to scream and shout. There is never a need to fight and be combative.

When you stand strong, with a silent, authentic compassion, you create conditions that bring about effortless cooperation from others.

This is not WEAKNESS; this is a SILENT STRENGTH that very few possess.

Be STILL. Be SILENT.

Be MASTERFULLY MYSTERIOUS.

When we become silent, like the sage on the mountain, we neutralize all conditions so that we may shape them as we desire, for we already know that there is nothing to combat in the nothingness but ourselves.

You are the calm waters
as well as the raging storm.

"I am strong, confident, and able to achieve anything I desire because I have chosen to take the advanced classes of life."

I Am Academic

Life may be difficult for you right now. You may wonder why your life is more difficult than others.

Know this: Life is nothing more than a classroom, and the classes you choose. Some choose basic math…

But you?

You chose calculus!

If you turned to this page…

Then you have been CHOSEN. You have been chosen to uphold and learn about the light within the darkness that bestows this planet. You have a job to do and being yourself is the only requirement.

Being a strong and faithful student of life is how the Presence empowers us and prepares us for GREATNESS.

You have been called upon
to make a difference. Stop wasting
time. Go now and be great.

"I am living fearlessly every
moment, knowing that
this is just one experience
of many to come."

I Am Eternal

When you realize death is only a transition to a different reality, it is then that you'll no longer fear dying...

Or living...for that matter. You are able to relax and embrace the ride of life for what it is...an experience.

Nothing more, nothing less.

Be fearless in your descent from this world knowing that you are not actually leaving, but arriving.

Heaven isn't up there. It is only here within the spectrum of our minds and hearts. It is not that we go somewhere, but yet transition into another dimension within the reality we are in now.

You are death and you are life.
You forever exist.

"I close my eyes and look within at the truth, for I know that when I seek knowledge from within, there is no reason to look outward."

I Am Intelligence

When you are looking for TRUTH outside of yourself, you miss out on the wisdom and miracles that are already within you.

How do I know?

Because I have learned to look within and see beyond this reality. You have the ability to see what most don't want to see. The answers to all the questions you have are not visible on the physical plane; they are within, where God is.

Know that when you look away from the physical world, you begin to see what you have been missing all along. You discover the Kingdom within. You discover Paradise.

When we look through the mind's eye, we will begin to see.

Intelligence comes from within.

"I surrender now and receive the abundant life God created for me."

I Am Surrender

At times you may feel all is lost…when you feel you can't go on any longer. That is the time to completely surrender and receive.

Just let go and let God take control. Release the burden, and then, wait patiently.

Life becomes easier and less exhausting with help. Always.

You need not be religious when asking for help from a Presence that knows you more than you know yourself. Strong people ask for help. Weak people stay silent in their EGO.

It is when we offer a silent surrender that we allow for a better life to be presented to us. A life that we could only dream about. Let go now and surrender.

You and the presence are onc.
You cannot be lost for long.

"I choose to live
the TRUTH."

I Am Truth

The imbalance in your life that you are experiencing has brought you to a crossroads.

You can either continue down the path that is taking you nowhere, or you can surrender…right now.

Then and only then, will you be guided out of the dark. It is when we are not living a life that resonates true within our heart and soul, do we become sick. The only person you are kidding is yourself. It is time to discover who you were meant to be…YOUR TRUTH.

When we find ourselves lost, we must acknowledge that we need help. And when we finally ask for help, we are able to release the huge burden that has weighed us down for so long. Then we can start to rest and recoup while letting God arrange the TRUTH…the life we desire.

Follow your truth
at the crossroads of life.

"I am the Thanksgiving that the world needs right now."

I Am Thank You

Today say "Thank You" all day. Say "Thank You" for everything you have now…even if it's not much.

Keep saying "Thank You" as much as you can today…

And by tomorrow, the Universe will give you more to be thankful for.

Know this: When you find yourself stuck for any reason, saying "Thank You" will release any block.

Being grateful for EVERTHING—

even what you do not desire—

will create a shift that will manifest miracles.

When we are experiencing anything negative and don't know what to do, just keep saying "Thank You" until it changes.

Thank You God for all You have given.
Thank You for all that You have done.

"I make a difference in the world just by being here. I am changing the world just by being me."

I Am Difference

No matter what you have done (or not done) while here on Earth, you have made a difference, just by being here.

Your Presence is more than enough to change the world for the better.

Thank You for being here.

Thank You for being You.

THANK YOU.

We must go and do what we were called upon to do. Go make more of a difference in this world. Go be YOU.

Remember, you are needed here
at this very moment in time.

"I forgive and release my past, knowing that all my new experiences allow me to become a better person."

I Am Unfolding

It is when you face the dark shadows fearlessly that you realize they are nothing more than past experiences you refuse to let go of.

Know this: Your future will not unfold until you embrace your past completely and then release it, knowing that it's just a learning experience.

Never be too hard on yourself. Stay focused, for the road to success that lies ahead wants you not to look in the rearview mirror, but only forward.

Take one day at a time. Be present in each moment. Act methodically and think clearly and stay focused. Don't rush or stress. Let everything flow.

And remember, when we are learning, we are always growing.

Your life is built upon your experiences...
All of them.

"I release the need to hold on to what no longer serves me, and set free my mind, body, and soul."

I Am Trinity

Purge all the junk from your diet.

Purge all the junk from your home.

Purge all the junk from your mind.

Purge all the junk from your life.

Then and only then will you attract everything you desire including, Heaven itself…

Remember LESS is MORE. Always.

Having minimal in your life, raises your energy so that you can be healthy, wealthy and joyful. Having too much will literally suffocate you.

It's time to go now and clean and purge, keeping only the absolute minimum in our surroundings. Then we will begin to feel a powerful energy shift.

You are not the baggage
that you carry.

"I am more than I know.
I AM."

I Am Identity

Your identity is not your career, job, status, wealth, character, persona, failure, self-righteousness, depression, illness, marriage, parenthood, or religious dogma.

Your identity is that of sitting still in the silence, listening to the voice within.

And when you hear the voice clearly, you will discover your "true" self apart from this world as we know it.

In order for us to "know thyself," we must "deny" self. And by that, we must let go of everything that has to do with the false self…letting go of EGO. Then…we become PRESENCE.

You are something of greatness other than who you are in this human reality.

"There is no separation because I am one with everyone and everything. I come from the same Source as all."

I Am Woven

Division means to separate… And when you separate, you single out…

When you are singled out, you are alone… And loneliness never accomplished anything.

When you separate yourself from The Creator and all that is, you cut off all lifelines. You detach from the very fabric that sustains you.

Everyone and Everything is intertwined within the ominous design. Once you understand this, you realize you were never alone and you have all that you need. You complete everything, including yourself.

When we isolate ourselves from each other, we become powerless which causes our minds and bodies suffer.

You complete everything when you
become one with everything.

"I move forward with confidence knowing there is a greater plan that I am a part of. All I have to do is be who I was created to be."

I Am Progress

Know this: Everything happens for a reason. There are absolutely no coincidences, whatsoever.

Everything is corresponding to the plan in motion. What plan is this? It is the plan you created before you came here. It is when you remember who you are and why you are here, does the plan complete itself.

If you do not remember, then ask the Presence to reveal what you already know within your heart.

When we begin to live our lives expecting to be guided by signs, symbols, and other forms of supernatural communication, then and only then do we become distracted from our Truth.

You know exactly who you are
and what you want. You just
need to be reminded.

"I am grateful to God for my precious body, which I respect and honor."

I Am Body

How you take care of your body is how you "Thank" your Creator for the precious life you were given.

How are you "Thanking" God?

If you refuse to take care of your body, then it will fail. If your body fails, you fail and then your life follows suit.

It's not about accepting yourself as you are, it's about becoming the masterpiece that God sculpted you to be.

Taking care of your physical "temple" starts always in the mind. Clean up and heal your thoughts and then you will begin to understand health as it should be.

When we are healthy, life flows naturally and effortlessly.

You only get one body per lifetime.

"I fully embrace all of my relationships as an integral part of my life, which makes me a better person."

I Am Relationships

Know this: Every relationship you experience gives you something to learn and grow from. It may not always be pleasant, but it will always make you stronger and better in the end.

Your worst adversary is your greatest teacher. Learn all you can from them with humility and gratitude, then move on. Otherwise, they will continue to cause friction until you finally get it.

Think about who is your biggest challenge right now. Who do you butt heads with the most? Who is constantly berating you? This is the person you need to pay close attention to.

Every person that comes into our life teaches us something about ourselves.

You are what your relationships become.

"I remain calm and steady during every storm because I control my emotions."

I Am Stillness

If you can weather the storm by remaining calm and neutral, no matter the duration or the turbulence, I promise you calmer waters will follow.

Believe you are the captain of your boat on the sea of life. By thinking positive and remaining calm at all times, you will eventually reach peaceful waters.

Remember, it's not about DOING; it's about THINKING. Think about what you desire and keep thinking about it until it divinely flows to you.

Stop trying to force a quick outcome when navigating a difficult situation in your life.

Once we let go of our obsessive paddling upstream, life will flow effortlessly to perhaps a new and better solution.

You can have all that you desire when you allow the desire to flow freely.

"I am at peace with all beginnings and endings because I know everything will eventually come full circle."

I Am Circle

With every beginning, there is an ending. And with every ending, there is a beginning. If you truly embrace this, you will forever be at peace.

Nothing remains the same. It is ever-changing according to your thoughts, beliefs and how you see the world.

If something ends, it's okay.

If something begins, it's okay.

When you can fully embrace this knowledge, all suffering will cease as you know it.

The ending that we may be experiencing right now, pay attention to it for it is creating an opening for something else to come along. Be open and embrace the change because it always leads to something better.

You are the ending because you are
the beginning, and everything in between.

"I serve and help others with dignity, refusing to compromise my self-worth."

I Am Service

Donating your time and serving others can be personally rewarding…and challenging. As I'm sure you already know, despite your best intentions, you cannot please everyone. And truthfully, you wouldn't want to. People-pleasing will get you nowhere but stuck in a reality that will block any appreciation and success from reaching you.

When you try to people-please, you create an energy around you that allows others to willfully take advantage of you. Even though some may appreciate your helpful efforts, others will abuse it.

When we serve others with a humble strength and gracious heart, knowing our high self-worth, we actually experience the gratification of giving.

Serving others is rewarding,
knowing that your self-worth
always rises to the task.

"I release all addictions and receive abundance now, for I know that anything that has control over me will block all blessings."

I Am Sober

Any addiction whatsoever that helps numb the pain, fear, or anger you are feeling, will also block any abundance, success or happiness coming to you.

When you are blind and fearful of what is in front of you, you are in a sense saying that you CAN'T, and therefore WON'T. It is easier to silence what you need to understand by hiding within the mask of addiction.

What don't you want to see? Yourself? Take each hour as it comes while you sit and go within. You will overcome. I promise.

The addictions that imprison us will disappear when we realize that we created them in order to avoid confronting what we need to understand.

Your life will begin to flow
effortlessly when you remove
the block of addiction.

"My power reflects my
worthiness, dignity
and confidence, knowing
that I AM who I AM."

I Am Power

Know this: You can't sell ANYTHING to ANYONE, if you don't know you. And when you don't know you, you can't believe in you EITHER.

In order for you and your endeavor to succeed, you must first know who you are and then start believing it. Only then can you sell it.

Look within your heart to discover you. If you don't like what you find, then change it.

Be authentic. Be humble. Be True. Then people will have something to believe in.

The moment we embrace who we are and what we stand for, that is when others will BUY into what we are SELLING.

You know exactly who you are. You have just forgotten. It is time to remember.

"I forgive myself and
release the rest because it
no longer serves my intention
to move forward."

I Am Forgetting

I t's not only forgiveness you need to practice. It's forgetting and releasing. The only person you ever need to forgive is yourself for letting others and situations disrupt your peaceful abundance.

It is when you choose to hold tightly on to something that caused you pain and dismantled your ego, that you find yourself unsure of how to free yourself from that memory.

We must do our best to forget about it and then move on. Once we can do this, we are able to live healthy, abundant and joyful lives that bring forth honor, dignity and self-worth.

Your forgiveness creates all conditions
that will help you through this life.

"I erase all negative memories that no longer serve me, knowing that they are mere illusions that have come and gone."

I Am Erasing

It is very important to let go of all animosity towards anyone or anything from your past if you want success and abundance to come to you.

By all means, you are not required to make amends of any kind, for the moment has come and gone. However, you must acknowledge it for what it is and then release it without regret.

When these unwanted memories of the past resurface, they become the dark shadows that you have created out of your lack of knowledge as to what is only fear that you have chosen to hold on to.

It is when we refuse to let go of any disgruntled moment in time that we keep that negative energy close to us, which in the end, poisons not only our bodies and minds but our life reality.

Your memories are creating your future.
Which ones are you holding on to?

"I speak my truth without fear, knowing that when my voice is heard, it changes not only others and the world, but it changes me."

I Am Voice

Stand up for what you believe in. Speak your voice and stand by it. When you bow down to others, afraid of the consequences, you are stating that you aren't important and your voice will go unheard.

However, you must look towards the Presence to guide you to that which you can speak TRUTH in order for others to HEAR your VOICE.

Be humble, but strong. Be compassionate, yet forthright. Be loving, yet discerning. Be hopeful, yet practical.

There will always come a time in our lives when we need to speak TRUTH to those who are lost and looking for guidance.

You are much more
than you say you are.

"I refrain from emotionally attaching myself to any situation or outcome."

I Am Detachment

Believe it or not, when you step back and let things just happen as they may—without any attachment or need for any outcome—it is then that everything falls perfectly into place.

You must realize that there is no object (thing) that you need…ever. Aside from survival needs, your other needs are met from within. The only problem that arises is when you see something and believe you need to have it.

Imagine, if you will, a white room with nothing in it. And let's say you were able to design that room as you chose. How would that room look? This is exactly what you can do with your entire life.

As we look beyond, into the NOTHINGNESS, we will then know that what we're looking for is already inside of us.

You are the veil that hides
the reality you desire.

"I am a blessing to all those
I come in contact with, knowing
that I am also blessed beyond
all I could imagine."

I Am Blessed

I f you want your life to change, if you truly want your circumstances to get better, then first and foremost, start by being a blessing to others.

ENCOURAGE them.

COMPLIMENT them.

LIFT them up.

HELP them feel good.

Then your blessings will come abundantly effortless, for what you put out there into the world, surely comes back to you tenfold.

When we need healing, go heal someone. When we need love, go love someone. When we need peace, go give someone peace. You get my point.

You are the blessing.

"I am allowing God to
demolish and reconstruct
a new life for me."

I Am Renewed

So you're at rock bottom right now...or at least it feels that way?

Which means there is nothing left to do but surrender. Just let go. Once you stop completely, it is then that God can start rebuilding your life better than it was.

By surrendering and letting go of what you think should be, you allow a grander design to be shown and established. The reason why you find yourself leveled out, is because you are trying to build faulty foundations based on your own understanding.

There is always a reason why we find ourselves and our lives upheaved all of a sudden. When we become comfortable with our surroundings, knowing deep down we have a grander purpose, we find that we are given a PUSH to remind us of just that.

You are only as good as the foundation
that you choose to have.

"I have the ability to communicate with God anytime I desire because I am authentic."

I Am Heard

Y ou don't have to pray lofty prayers to speak to your Creator or those on the other side. Just be yourself. Talk to God as you would talk to your friend. But know this: Remain true and forthright in your communication, therefore you waste not what is important.

There are times when falling to your knees is the only thing you can think of doing. Those moments will allow you to completely surrender and let go of all the burdens you have been carrying for so long. This is prayer being answered as well.

When we find the NEED to pray, it shouldn't be out of NEED in the first place, for we already have what we NEED. Instead, use these moments to give thanks for whatever is causing imbalance in life, or the lives of others. Gratitude is what all prayers should express..."THANK YOU, for listening to my prayer."

You are what makes prayer possible,
for you are the prayer itself.

"I place my complete trust in God, who directs the steps that I humbly and graciously take."

I Am Trust

If you put your complete trust in others…you will ultimately be very disappointed, EVERY TIME.

If you put your complete trust in the Creator…your trust will be rewarded, EVERY TIME.

Stay solely focused on God for help with your business, relationships, health and everything in your life.

Trust God and yourself completely. Sound selfish? Maybe? I urge you to try this. And you will see, that THOSE who you trusted before will never match the unconditional trust of God.

It is when we are told to look to God, we must look within and not without.

You, me, everyone… "In God we trust."
Be thankful for that alone.

"I am the miracle
because I am the light
in which everything else
becomes revitalized."

I Am Miracle

Do you need to be religious to receive miracles? Absolutely not.

You don't have to be anything, because in "truth" you are the miracle. And you need to do nothing to be that miracle.

When you realize that you were created to be a powerful being who upholds the LIGHT on Earth by just being the LIGHT, life takes on a whole new meaning, one based upon TRUTH.

Religion is that of which people make it to be most of the time: Safe, Comforting, a Community, their Heritage, a Mask, an Excuse, a Scapegoat, etc.

When we are able to see past any dogma that may distort our spiritual connection, we are able to experience God from a realistic standpoint. And with that, we can have a REAL relationship with God.

You are the miracle and that
will never change.

"I am living naturally, as my Creator intended. It is when I am in touch with nature that I become alive and powerful."

I Am Nature

Those who are the most:
    Healthy
    Happy
    Fulfilled
    Successful
are the ones who live completely in nature, away from:
    Pollution
    Noise-chaos
    Technology
    Modern conveniences

The dangers you face in this modern world are astronomical. You are constantly being bombarded with toxins from chemicals being sprayed in the air daily. Unnatural energy disrupts your body's natural chemistry.

When we reconnect and immerse ourselves in nature, we experience renewed joy.

Your mind, body, and soul were meant to
live and thrive in a natural world.

"My life and everything around it flows easily and effortlessly because I have the power, as God intended, to remove all negative energy from myself and the world."

I Am Light

To attract all you desire, you must remove the negative energy that attaches to you daily. All you have to do is imagine a cloud of energy around you.

Now clap your hands and wave them around. Repeat:

"In the darkness, the light prevails. I command all negative energy to be gone at once."

Now surround yourself with a golden light. Works every time.

Every day and every night we need to remove unwanted energy. Doing this will actually attract more abundance, health, and all that we desire.

You have all the power
you need right now.

"Everything I desire chases me because I know that I am worthy of having all that I desire."

I Am Desire

When you chase anything…it will run. ALWAYS. Sit still without a care…then everything will come to you effortlessly.

Act as if you need nothing. Only then will everything come to you.

When you become desperate for anything such as money, people, circumstances or change, you send out a powerful signal saying you are unworthy.

Sit still and KNOW that we can attract ANYTHING and EVERYTHING.

The world was created with thought.
You have the same power.

"I am equal because I stand on the same ground as everyone else. Therefore I live as powerfully as everyone else."

I Am Equality

No one is more…
Privileged
Favored
Blessed
Special
Right

…than anyone else. People are all the same when they leave this world; once you understand this, all prejudice becomes obsolete. If you learn anything…learn this.

This isn't about race, religion, politics, beliefs, practices, rules, regulations, opinions, status, power, greed, poverty or wealth.

We are ALL cut from the same cloth of God. And it is each person's choice to either respect and honor everyone, or discolor that cloth with prejudice towards others.

Your ability to see differently is
merely the blindness that has
caused you to stumble.

"Today I become the
person that I've always
wanted to be, the miracle
God created me to be."

I Am Today

Today:
I will not complain, but instead give a compliment. I will not become frustrated, but instead be compassionate. I will not feed my ego, but instead show my humility. I will not ask, "What's in it for me?" but instead ask, "How can I help?"

I will not hold a grudge, but instead, practice forgiveness. I will not take things for granted, but instead show gratitude for everything. I will not be knocked down, but instead rise and stand tall.

We have the incredible ability to change…every single day.

Today is your moment to change
and make a difference.

"I am wealthy already
because I know I am
worthy of wealth, as my
Creator intended."

I Am Prosperous

You can play the lottery all you want…but if you have "poverty thoughts," your efforts will be futile. Start speaking, thinking, feeling and acting as if you have won already.

Know this: Money is only energy. Nothing more and nothing less. You have the ability to obtain all that you need without MONEY, if you choose to do so. You can't pray for money. It doesn't work like that. But you can pray for what you want that money could buy.

It is in the KNOWING that we are prosperous already and that wealth is manifesting in our lives.

You are the divine creative law.

"I release all regrets as if they were coins tossed into a wishing well, knowing that when I release the weight, I am free to fly."

I Am Regretless

Regrets are like unwanted pocket change. You're not sure what to do with it, yet you carry it everywhere or keep it in various places around your home. Instead of spending it or just getting rid of it, you hang on to it out of habit.

You do the same with regrets. Regrets are just loose pocket change that you have accumulated and refuse to release.

If you continue to hang on to them, they become dead weight that only weighs you down with something that isn't worth much.

When we release our regrets and empty our pockets of the emotional weight that holds us back, our lives will have room for more than just chump change.

Your regrets are keeping you
from something better.

"I take full responsibility for everything I do, knowing that blaming others only makes me someone I'm ashamed of becoming…a coward."

I Am Responsibility

The Blame Game:

You blame her,
    She blames him.
He blames that,
    She blames this.
They blame you,
    The world blames God.
You blame them,
    They blame us.
On and on,
    On and on...
...which leaves absolutely NO ONE responsible for ANYTHING.

When we honestly identify responsibility, it allows us to resolve, release, and move forward...instead of continually kicking the can further down the road.

You need not say more.

"I live a powerful life because
I am free from the fear that
plagues most. I am fearless for
I have nothing to lose, yet I
remain steadfast knowing that
I have everything to gain."

I Am Fearlessness

FEAR will keep you from living your dreams.

FEAR will keep you from being a successful millionaire.

FEAR will keep you from leaving your mark in this world.

FEAR will hold you down until you're gone.

When you live FEARLESSLY, you are able to harness the power to achieve and grow.

The only way you can conquer fear is to face it HEAD ON. Now go, go find what scares you and stand up to it.

Know this: When we face our fears, we realize that they are nothing more than a state of mind that keeps us from grabbing hold of the dream we have always wanted to come true.

You are the only thing
that frightens yourself.

"I am free as God intended because I refuse to let anything or anyone control me. I release the chains of imprisonment that confine my life."

I Am Boundless

What CONTROLS you?

Your cell phone? The Internet? Your TV? Video games? Nicotine? Alcohol? Drugs? Racism? Fear?

You should pause here, think, and take a deep breath before continuing with this list. You may have more to add.

Junk food? Friends? Family? Spouse? The government? Your job? Others? Options? Beliefs? The church? Religion? Pride?

We weren't created for anything or anyone to have control over us. Perhaps NOW is the time for us to break free and fly?

Stop restraining yourself.
Set yourself free.

"I am not only becoming a better human, I am perfecting my soul with every new experience."

I Am Spontaneous

Know this: You have and will have many unexpected experiences in life. Each one will bring new opportunities, challenges, and growth.

No one is keeping score or checking red marks for the way you respond to new experiences. And, no one is giving out gold stars either. Once you realize that there is no REPORT CARD for the way you live your life at any given time, you then become free to LIVE your life as you CHOOSE.

Go and make mistakes. Go and fail a few times. Go and be silly and stupid. Go and be carefree. Go and be risky. Go and be crazy fun. Go and be powerful. Go and be childlike. Go and be successful. Go and LIVE LIFE.

You are the childlike spirit that
God wants you to be.

"I forgive myself first, knowing that when I do, all else is forgiven, which leaves nothing left to forgive."

I Am First

The only person you ever need to forgive is yourself. Forgive yourself for letting others make you feel anything less than you are. Forgive yourself for letting others disrupt your peace and happiness. Forgive yourself for letting others live your life as they choose.

Forgive now, and you and the rest of the world will be forgiven. Then and only then, can you become ALL.

I have seen forgiveness heal cancer, arthritis, colds, and many other illnesses and diseases. Forgiveness is the ultimate power that we possess.

When we forgive ourselves first and foremost, we are actually forgiving the rest of the world, as well as God.

You have not forgotten how to forgive.
You just need to remember it is only
yourself that needs forgiveness.

"I freely express my feelings and openly release them, knowing that the world will understand that I am sharing, purging, and naturally detoxing my mind and body so that I will remain healthy."

I Am Feeling

If you feel like crying…then truly cry.

If you feel like being mad…then truly get mad.

If you feel like laughing…then truly laugh.

If you are overflowing with joy…then share it with others.

This is a wonderful gift of being a human. But with the gift of feelings comes a word of warning.

Don't ever hold back your feelings, for therein lies a problem.

When you become your feelings you allow them to take over rational thought, which disengages you from your natural ability to discern as to what is truly important from an intellectual standpoint, thus creating emotional instability.

When we are able to freely express our feelings while totally surrendering to those feelings, we cleanse our bodies and souls in order to start fresh once again.

Your feelings are indicators of what
is truly important to you.

"I am strong enough to handle anything, for I know that nothing is too great for me to overcome as long as I just keep going."

I Am Stronghold

There are days I don't want to wake UP. There are moments when I want to give UP. There are weeks I want to throw my hands UP.

And then there are the years that have passed to where I am still here…standing UP.

Take each MOMENT one at a time. Take each HOUR one at a time. Take each DAY one at a time. Soon you will find that you were fine all along.

I know what you are going through, for I and many many others have been there several times. It is a part of life and you will get through it.

Know this: Every challenge or difficulty only tests our resolve, so in the end, we become stronger. Just Keep Going.

You are the strength that will
carry you to the end.

"I need absolutely NO approval
from anyone for I am powerful,
successful, and talented
as I was born to be."

I Am Sturdy

WHO said you weren't good enough?
WHO said you wouldn't succeed?
WHO said to play it safe?
WHO said you weren't smart enough?
WHO said that your dreams would never come true?
Whoever "THEY" are…

They can only control their lives and only you can control your life.

Remember, there is no WHO, only YOU.

Know this: There are people who instinctively criticize, as a way to validate themselves. We become sturdy by respecting our TRUTH and validating ourselves.

Don't forget the person that
you have forgotten…you.

"I am achieving my dreams no matter what, and I will not stop until we find each other. Then I will dream of another... and another!"

I Am Determination

If you sit around waiting for some other time to go after your dreams and the life you desire to live...

Then you might as well plan your departure from this world.

The only perfect time is NOW. Because there is only the present, and after that, time doesn't exist.

Know this: The dreams you have in your mind are REAL. And if you keep thinking about them daily, you give them life.

We must realize that when nothing seems to be happening in our lives, our dreams are closer than we realize. Just Keep Believing.

You are the dream that resides
in the present moment.

"My need to constantly feel that I am special is a mere insecurity that serves no purpose in my life. I am powerful, and powerful people don't need validation from others."

I Am Enough

Why do you need someone to tell you that you are special?

And if they did…would you believe it anyway?

Basing your worth on someone else's validation is insanity at its best.

The most damaging thought you can have is the fact that you are not worthy, or unworthy for that matter.

How are you not worthy? You were created from the same God as everyone else. It makes no sense.

I don't care where you came from or where you are now…you have a choice. Choose to go out and do what you need to do…what you want to do.

We have every right to live as we choose. No one is holding us back, other than ourselves.

Your self worth is only as good as
your limitless imagination.

"I create my own path to
success knowing that when
I free myself from the crowd
I am able to soar to great heights
beyond all I could imagine."

I Am Solo

If you follow the crowd…you will get lost in the crowd. If you get lost in the crowd…you will perish in the crowd.

Successful people step completely away from the crowd. They stand alone, fearless and confident, knowing they were made for something greater than the crowd.

Today…fearlessly step aside from the crowd and confidently…WALK AWAY.

Right now, look around you into the crowd that surrounds you. What do you SEE? Take a really good LOOK.

Know that when we finally step aside, out on our own way, our success will launch us beyond anything that we could have ever imagined.

You were meant to stand alone.

"I now let go of the need for change, knowing it will always come on time."

I Am Embrace

I f you are experiencing an unpleasant time in your life right now, then be patient. It will change. I Promise.

If you are experiencing a pleasant time in your life right now, then deeply cherish every minute of it.

Time is nonexistent in TRUTH, therefore you are standing where you have always been standing. The only thing that changes is your perception. The illusion that you call your present reality, is the thought that you had in the past. What are you thinking now? Figure it out, because you are creating your future. NOW.

Know that nothing stays the same.

Change is inevitable. Embrace it with an open mind. Then and only then will we have the courage to experience what we desire...effortlessly.

You are the change that you seek.
Nothing more, nothing less.

"I take the step forward, knowing my Creator meets me halfway every time."

I Am Movement

If you are waiting around for someone to come rescue you, you will be waiting for an eternity.

However, if you get up and get going, the Creator will meet you more than halfway.

Start right now by sitting still in the quiet. Hold within your mind of what you want. Even if you have doubt, think about exactly what you want right now. Stay focused on that.

God will rearrange the universe in order for the very thing we desire to come true, as long as it is good within our hearts. I promise.

You are your own savior by causing movement towards the effect.

"I spark joy in my heart
from activities and memories
that shift my energy."

I Am Joyful

When all else fails, when you have nowhere to turn and you have no idea how to pull yourself up out of the hopelessness, grab hold of something good, if not for a moment.

Watch a movie. Read a book. Listen to music. Walk in nature. This will shift your energy.

Right now, think of a time that you would relive over and over if you could.

Really envision and recall the memory that made you feel alive. Keep playing it through your mind and I promise you will feel better.

Remember that the minute we change our thoughts, our reality changes instantly.

You have the power to change any reality
that you are in. Right now.

"I am raising and empowering my child to be the best they can be, so that they can achieve their own success."

I Am Guardian

Remember as a parent or guardian, your responsibility is to prepare your child to fully succeed in the world today. It is a true sacrifice that brings the greatest rewards to all.

You gave them life. Now teach them how to create an amazing life of their own. You owe this to them.

You are your child's teacher for becoming successful in life. Make sure you empower them for that success.

We have the power and obligation to help our children discover and develop their gifts, so they may go out and become everything they can imagine becoming.

A child's success is only as good as they think it is. Teach them well.

"I accept and offer constructive criticism so that I, as well as others, can go beyond any limits."

I Am Constructive

The world today, has become too politically correct. Being too PC puts a fluffy Band-Aid on the truth. Which in turn, masks the cause, leaving no cure.

It naively protects humans from much-needed constructive criticism that helps them become greater than what they are now.

Political correctness creates mediocrity on all levels.

We are not being ruthless nor unkind when expressing whatever is on our minds. It is having the confidence and compassion to speak as to what is TRUTH—without fluffing the TRUTH—as not to coddle those who are fearful of themselves.

You are strong enough to
be direct and honest.

"I am authentic to the core, for I know that when I allow someone else to speak my voice, I lose respect for myself."

I Am Individual

You must understand that you were created to be COMPLETELY different than anyone else. You were created to stand OUT.

When you try to be like others, you erase your authenticity and individuality. It is harder to be like someone else than to be your own true self.

When you compare ourselves to others, thus wanting to emulate them for reasons that you don't know, you lose sight of the distinctiveness that brings forth a certain knowing that you are truly like no other.

Remember, every one of us brings something special to the table of life. If we didn't, life would be boring. DO YOU WANT TO BE BORING?

Your difference is what sets you
apart from the herd.

"I am a guiding light in a world that craves inspiration and direction."

I Am Insight

When you feel as if the world has gone mad and let you down…

When you feel as if you are standing alone…

That is the time for you to shine and become stronger than ever.

The time is now, for you to become a beacon for the light in order to obliterate the darkness. If you are reading this right now, you have been chosen to do as such.

Stop hiding behind everyone else's fear and insecurities. Walk confidently with a bright light. The world will be better than it once was.

You are the lone wolf that
the world needs.

"I allow my life to fit perfectly as God intended, knowing I was created to be different from everyone else, just like a fingerprint."

I Am Distinction

Trying to put a square peg in a round hole is insanity at its best.

When you try to force your life into a mold that doesn't fit, all inevitably fails. What is meant to be fits effortlessly, perfect.

Know this: Before you set out to visit this physical reality called Earth, a divine plan was in place to guide you. Unfortunately—like most—you forgot that plan and now you are going around without a map seeking the life you were meant to live.

Sit still in the quiet and ask God to send you a copy of the map so you can reconnect with the life you have always imagined.

Remember, each of us is one of a kind, an original piece, created to be unlike any other in this world.

You are a work of distinction like no other.
Your fingerprint will never be duplicated.

"I live a life that is honest to my TRUTH that others respect and look towards for leadership."

I Am Honesty

The disease or illness you are experiencing now is your body's way of telling you that you are out of balance, which most likely is caused by not living the life that resonates in your heart's desire.

Illness and disease seek out those who are weak within their mindset as to what truly is.

And what is that TRUTH? It is the fact that you were designed to be COMPLETELY healthy and never to fall ill for any reason.

God is good. And God is all. If this is so, then you are good and you are all, including perfect health.

When we live honestly at all times, wellness becomes our path.

The cure you seek starts with
the truth in your heart.

"I enjoy the wonder of seeing the world as a child again because I have let go of the need to listen to adults that refuse to see the world as it truly is... a place of magic."

I Am Childlike

Stop taking things so seriously. None of this matters in the larger scheme of life, here and beyond.

Be childlike for one day and you will soon discover what is truly important. You will discover Heaven.

When you become childlike, a whole new world of wonder opens up and you let go of all the troubles that adults create.

Study children and you will understand what it means to be perfect as God intended.

When we take life too seriously, we give up our power and end up becoming boring, grumpy, cynical people, mad at others for all the unhappiness in life.

Happiness will come when you
become childlike again.

"I remain calm and hopeful when the tide goes out, for I know it will always come back."

I Am Tide

I know you are hurting right now and you feel as if you can't go on. Everything seems hopeless and you can't find any relief.

Know this: The tide will turn, I promise.

Just hold on. If I can make it, you can too. Just like the tide of the ocean, when you think that everything is gone, that is when it comes rushing back in, perfectly in time.

Know that you are fully equipped to go the long haul. And in the end, when you have reached the top, you can say…I DID IT!

We see the tide fall and then we see the tide rise, each time restoring life to the shore. We must realize that nothing can erode our spirit without replenishing it with renewed strength.

You were not created to give up.

"My heart is guiding me
to a powerful life."

I Am Heart

Your heart is the TRUTH.

If you allow your head to overrule your heart, it will confuse the Universe, and you'll receive confusing results.

We can't say this any simpler. Life will manifest the TRUTH residing in the heart. We must be brave and courageous to acknowledge this.

Your heart is the true brain of the body.

"I embrace my past with acceptance and understand that this is all a learning experience for the growth I need to expand my consciousness."

I Am Learning

S top running from your past.

In order for you to heal, cleanse yourself, and be free from your past. Look at it head on, then embrace it for what it was… A learning experience. Nothing more, nothing less.

Now that it no longer controls you, there's no need to be afraid, shamed, guilty, regretful, angry, sad, or condemned. EVER.

Once you have completely accepted your past with a gentle peace, release it and let it go like the wind.

Life is meant to enjoy, live in peace, and most of all, EXPERIENCE.

When we try to bury or destroy the past, we are burying and destroying our identity. We must learn that we can overcome our dark moments and still move forward to appreciate the glory of life.

Don't let your past control your present and future.

"I create powerful change by dreaming large, knowing that God already has big dreams for me."

I Am Dreamstate

Those who think small dreams, create little change. Those who think large dreams, create massive change.

If your world has been completely turned upside down, do not panic, for this is a good thing. It's time to dream large.

Change is coming to you and you will begin to see the fruit of your thoughts.

When we Dream Utterly Ominous, Untouchably Amazing, Astonishingly Abundant Dreams, we open the floodgates to a life of Unlimitedly Free Imagination and Potential. Phew!

You are the dream and the
dream is you.

"I am thankful that
God walks with me."

I Am The I Am

Thank you for walking with me God…for I know you are there when I stumble…just as you are there when I fly.

Thank you for walking with me God…for I know you are there when my heart is broken…just as you are there when I am in love.

Thank you for walking with me God…for I know you are there when I fail…just as you are there when I succeed.

Thank you for walking with me God…for I know you are there when I am in the valley…just as you are there when I am on top of the mountain.

Thank you for walking with us God…for we know you'll be there when we are about to leave this Earth…just as you'll be standing there when we arrive in Heaven.

You are never alone.
Ever.

The Gift

Our Creator created us to live our best here on Earth. Everything needed to sustain life on this planet has been furnished. Our bodies are perfect as they were created, as well as our minds. The Earth itself is perfect as it was created. And with that, we are able to do, be, and have all that we desire.

However, there is but one more thing God gave us that I call a "gift." A gift that allows us to CREATE our reality just from our thoughts, words and feelings.

This gift I speak of is available to ALL of us. Many have spoken about this gift. And no, you do not have to be religious, privileged or even remotely intelligent to possess this gift. You just need to embrace it and, most importantly, BELIEVE that it works. I am not going to explain how it works or why it works. You don't need to know for it to work. Truthfully, just know that it does.

As I have said earlier, you must do the work, for it to work. But know this, when you do the work right the first time, it doesn't seem like work at all and the results are brilliant.

You are being asked to try this for a least two weeks. You must be consistent and you must have an open mind.

Every night when you retire to bed, as you are laying there, I want you to focus on this Prayer.

The Prayer

My body is perfection
Thank You God

My wealth is enormous
Thank You God

My talents are craved
Thank You God

My relationships are authentic
Thank you God

My home is paradise
Thank You God

My intuition is powerful
Thank You God

My life is a wonderful dream
Thank You God

Keep repeating it silently in your head as you drift off. Visualize in your mind good thoughts of any desire that relates to the Prayer. Feel the feelings of what you see. Stay focused on that alone and nothing else. That's it. Do this and I promise you that your reality will begin to change.

When you understand this gift and how it will change your entire life, you can begin to create your own affirmations to bring about whatever you desire.

Affirmations must be precisely constructed to be effective so that they detail the desired condition as current reality. Be sure to pay close attention to your surroundings for any signs, symbols, experiences, changes, dreams and upheavals that occur.

Each affirmation MUST be spoken. Throughout this book, the affirmations I have provided are specifically structured to implant the realization of their intent. Affirmations may also be structured to end with a proclamation of realization that states, "And so it is." For example: "I AM HEATHLY. AND SO IT IS."

Catherine Ponder is one of the most prolific prosperity writers of our time and her books are filled with examples of specific affirmations. If you need assistance, I recommend her classic, *The Dynamic Laws of Prosperity* (ISBN: 9780875165516), available on devorss.com or from other booksellers.

The Ending

We are in interesting times here on Earth. Some days the world is unrecognizable. We have become so far advanced with technology, yet we are more disconnected now than ever before.

Faith and a sense of hope are at an all-time low. And our personal connection with our Creator is diminishing at a rapid rate. Our lack of caring and compassion has hardened many hearts.

The willingness to humbly serve others has gone by the wayside. And those who selflessly serve to protect, we no longer honor or respect.

We fight and resist everything around us, assuming we are in control. Then we soon realize we were never in control to begin with, thus giving up our true freedom and the ability to discern what TRUTH is.

It is in those moments of uncertainty, we find ourselves pleading to God…"Help us." Yet the silence becomes deafening, as there is no answer in return. I believe the Universe is about balance.

Right now, we are at the tipping of the scales. We have reached a crucial impasse, creating a choice for us. "Do we become the blessing to this planet or, inevitably, its demise?"

And with that, the answer is unequivocally ours to decide as humans who care about the future of Earth.

As I am finishing the writings of this book, my life has gone through another transition—much like all of us I suspect—which is why these Messages within will bring a certain clarity as to why we are experiencing this moment in time.

The balance I speak of has brushed its Presence upon the world just enough to jolt our natural awakening, leading us to a better understanding as to;

"Who we are," "Why we are here," and "The purpose we must fulfill."

We need to understand that we are ONE and by separating the collective by choice and not living our "Truth" as that collective—as well as ourselves—we create an imbalance that can cause such devastation.

Recently, we have just witnessed what this imbalance can do. It is the ripple effect of our past that has come back to remind us of what is TRULY important. So how do we change this?

We can begin changing the world by changing our-selves FIRST and FOREMOST. Only then, can we create the life we truly desire.

Is this about religion? No.

Am I religious? No.

Do I believe in God? Yes. How could I not? I've had enough experiences to confirm my belief.

Do I know all that there is to know about God? No. None of us do.

But here's what I do know: We are not as in con-trol as we think we are. Maybe that is why so many feel out of control. We must acknowledge that there is something greater by allowing God to create the life we could only imagine.

The Thank You

I want to thank each one of you for joining me on this journey and being open to the wisdom within these pages.

The Messages are simple, yet powerful. They helped me more than I can say. They actually saved my life. Know this: Life was meant to be simple and natural, not fast, technical, or mechanical as we have made it be.

It is my wish that you will have found some clarity, strength and peace amongst the darkness and chaos that surrounds us on this Earth. You will have your good days and bad, as I still do. It is part of God's ominous plan.

Remember, God chose you to come here.

But know this: You are much more than the physical being that you see in the mirror. You are the Divine, capable of extraordinary things.

I want to thank the Presence for being ever so patient, gracious, forgiving, merciful, loving and bold with me while I continue to learn and grow. I am truly

Grateful for this gift called LIFE. Thank You for the Words of Wisdom that flow through me.

I Love You God,
Stephanie Reef

The Author

Stephanie Reef is a practicing metaphysician and healer of Christ Consciousness teachings and Kahuna healing practices. Her ability to see, hear and feel the energy from others and the environment allows her to diminish negative, stagnant, or earth-bound spirit energy that is causing illness, disease, emotional blocks, and disruption in your physical body, money, relationships, and surrounding environment.

Stephanie was born and raised in Denver, Colorado, and feels an affinity towards nature and the West. She lives as a minimalist and still puts pencil to paper when writing her books. You can email Stephanie at:

stephaniereefhealer@yahoo.com